UNLIMITING YOUR BELIEFS

UNLIMITING YOUR BELIEFS

Seven Keys to Greater Success in
Your Personal and Professional Life
Told Through My Journey to the
Toughest Race in the World

KAREN BROWN

NEW YORK

LONDON • NASHVILLE • MELBOURNE • VANCOUVER

UNLIMITING YOUR BELIEFS

Seven Keys to Greater Success in Your Personal and Professional Life

Told Through My Journey to the Toughest Race in the World

Published in New York, New York, by Morgan James Publishing. Morgan James is a trademark of Morgan James, LLC. www.MorganJamesPublishing.com

The Morgan James Speakers Group can bring authors to your live event. For more information or to book an event visit The Morgan James Speakers Group at www.TheMorganJamesSpeakersGroup.com.

ISBN 9781683504160 - paperback
ISBN 9781642790641 - case laminate
ISBN 9781683504177 - eBook
Library of Congress Control Number: 2017900725

Cover Design by: Rachel Lopez
www.r2cdesign.com

Interior Design by: Paul Curtis

In an effort to support local communities, raise awareness and funds, Morgan James Publishing donates a percentage of all book sales for the life of each book to Habitat for Humanity Peninsula and Greater Williamsburg.

Get involved today! Visit
www.MorganJamesBuilds.com

DEDICATION

To all the strong female role models who were a shining example of what could be achieved—starting with my mother Cammie, my Great Aunt Mary, and Julie Moss. And to all of the folks out there who are wondering what they can achieve.

TABLE OF CONTENTS

KEY FOUR
HIRE A COACH

KEY FIVE
DO WHAT IT TAKES / SCHEDULE = GOALS

KEY SIX
"NO" DISCIPLINE

KEY SEVEN
HIT YOUR GOALS, ENJOY THE VICTORY & SET NEWGOALS, DREAM AGAIN

ACKNOWLEDGMENTS

Each one of these people played a part in my journey. Each one of you knows in your own heart what you did to help me. I have enormous gratitude for your help. It is the most precious gift in the world to help someone realize a dream that leads them to live out their purpose, their potential.

My sister Ruby Purdy and best friend Crystal Seeley are my most staunch supporters: Alicia Kratt, Marge Kammerer, the Team Sistas!

The Keller Williams family of leaders, agents and team leaders including Gary Keller, the agents at the KWRS office, and team leaders in the KW Colorado Region.

My editor Mary Ann Tate saw this book for all it could be, and my assistant Carrie Ruddick treated this project so personally. Your detailed eyes were exactly what I needed. My publisher Morgan James and author relations manager Tiffany Gibson patiently answered all my questions and brought the book to fruition. I also thank my original book team.

The stars of the sport and the network of people in the sports arena who inspired and supported me and other athletes to reach our own potential: Julie Moss, Chrissie Wellington, Rich Roll, Brandon del Campo, Bob Cranny, Alpha

Bicycles, Kompetitive Edge, TriBella, and the volunteers at the Ironman World Championship 2012.

The countless friends and family members who always believed in and supported me: Cammie Oliver, T.S., Suzanne Yoder, Keith Alba, John Prescott, Jenn Morgan, Brian Smith, Joe Rothchild, Dr. Marci, Dr. Rob, Heather Kokx, Beth Davis, Fred Nehring, Chris Martel, Lynette Chase, Karen and Randy Morrow, Jay Papasan, Todd Nelson, and Jesse Sund.

FOREWORD

When I first met Karen Brown, it was five weeks before the Ironman World Championships in Kona, Hi, September 2012. Upon meeting her, I immediately saw her enormous vision, excitement, and determination to realize her 30-year dream of competing in Kona. Even though this was all-consuming for her, and she was coming to see me because of a painful right hamstring that could've stopped her in the race, she would not let fearful or negative thoughts derail her. I knew right then and there she would be successful because of her attitude and thoughts.

I have some experience with the Ironman World Championships, having competed there two times as a former age group elite Ironman triathlete. With this personal experience, as well as treating many professional and top-level athletes, I have seen that mindset and attitude are everything. The body will follow what the mind tells it to do, right or wrong, good or bad. In her journey to Kona, Karen discovered that 90% of ability to perform came from mindset and 10% from physical ability and application.

As we progressed through our weekly sessions, Karen related her incredible story of having not much more than a big dream and a determined will. She learned many valuable lessons along the way, such as the importance of thinking and doing things differently. If you want to get to a place you have never been before, you must expand your comfort zone and be in touch with your body and mind. Know that in every fiber of your body you have what it takes to accomplish your dream and visualize that dream every day.

In my business, I come face to face with people every day who make decisions—decisions that enable them to do things they want, or decisions that stop them from those things. Karen's story is a shining example of what all of us can do to align ourselves with what we want to accomplish, be the best version of ourselves and find out what we are truly capable of achieving.

Now that I've had the opportunity to know Karen better, I have seen that she has the heart of an everyday champion. She took her achievement in Kona and built on it, sharing it with others so that they may find their true potential and take their path. It is this kind of person that changes the world, one person at a time.

Bob Cranny, Physical Therapist
Owner, Altitude Physical Therapy and Sports Medicine
Ten-time Ironman Finisher
Two-time Ironman World Championship Finisher

INTRODUCTION

The Edge of My Comfort Zone

I used to go through life with an indistinct, hazy approach. I thought that by being easy and laid back, everything would somehow or other be taken care of.

Then I realized that approach would not get me where I wanted to go. It would get me where others wanted to go. That revelation came at age 23 after I had been blindly working my way toward becoming a military wife. I was in a long-distance, committed relationship with John, an Air Force service member who was very ambitious. Marriage was something I had always wanted, and I thought we would marry. Then I realized I did not want to become a military wife. I had big career ambitions of my own—to be the store manager of a high-end women's retail boutique. When I was promoted to that position, I knew that marrying John would mean I would spend my life moving from station to station. I would follow his aspirations and let mine become secondary. All at once, I realized I didn't want that life.

The experience served as an eye-opener. It led me to see what I wanted and to go after it. Pretty simple concept—simple, but not easy, like much of life.

Then came the feeling that I had something far bigger inside me that I could contribute or accomplish—but I didn't know what it was. The uncertainty of that elusive "bigger thing" brought about the somewhat sick feeling of knowing I was living within my "safe" and "easy" boundaries doing what I had always done, and being comfortable to the point of stagnation. I have always found when I'm not learning and growing, I'm stagnating.

Don't get me wrong. During this time I was moving up at work and was very physically active, competing in races of various kinds and trying new sports and techniques. Problem was, none of them stretched me beyond my limits. All kept me in my safe, comfy zone.

Until I thought about the Ironman World Championship, the toughest race in the world.

I began to look at my comfort zone as a rubber band with endless stretch-ability. I could go to the edge of my comfort, then stretch a little bit more and a little bit more each time. Before I began training for Ironman, I would look at the edge of my comfort zone as a cliff. I would choose to do what scared me, but only so far. I wouldn't go beyond that point. I'd temporarily alleviate my feelings of insecurity or inadequacy, then I'd feel better about myself for a little while. But those feelings would still nag at me. If I challenged myself too much and got too close to the edge, I felt like I would fall off.

Self-doubt is so commonplace and inconspicuous, we often overlook it; we don't even register its presence. To quiet my relentless self-doubts, I added plenty of miscellaneous tasks and "shiny-object" distractions to occupy my mind. I would focus on the wrong things and get myself off track so I could avoid that unsettling feeling of inadequacy from staying motionless at the edge my comfort zone.

Amidst my own self-doubts, there was this terrifying aspect of expanding my comfort zone and this question: Can I do what I'm considering doing? That question emanated from deep inside, along with What will others think? Or to be more precise—it's really what I thought others would think of me. Expanding my comfort zone also begged the question: What will it mean to me going forward?

In other words, if I couldn't do what I was setting out to do, maybe I was not as great as I thought I was.

This is a human phenomenon. All of this happens in a split-second thought process. We merge with our limiting beliefs and accept them as fact. It's how most of us live until we stop to question ourselves.

When I ran the Pikes Peak Ascent, I learned something helpful. This was a half-marathon up a 14,000-foot mountain on a narrow trail. It was completely within my comfort zone because I had hiked it many times and was a good runner. I'd seen the short list of athletes who did the full marathon. They were the names of elite athletes—a higher level than me. I began to allow myself to think about how these people could do things I couldn't wrap my head around, like the full marathon of the Pikes Peak Ascent. I had practiced for the race by running down from the top a few times. The pounding on my muscles caused by going downhill for 13 miles made me so sore I couldn't walk down stairs for a week and had to basically "fall" onto the toilet. I couldn't figure out how the marathoners in that race could do both the up and down. It seemed so far out of my realm of reality.

Up to this point in my life, I had allowed myself to get to a point of uncomfortable thinking about something like this, and then just write it off, as if it were basically un-doable for the common person. I'd rationalize that only those super-human beings like Matt Carpenter—who had a 60 percent bigger lung capacity than normal—could do it. This gave me a reason to dismiss thinking any further about how it could be done. And ultimately, how I could do it.

During the Pikes Peak Ascent half marathon, I gave myself permission to continue thinking about how they did it. This time I went a bit further, too. I began to ask myself, How could I do that? What if I tried? What if I could do it? What if that's inside me? What if I'm not pushing myself as far as I can? This was a huge shift in my thinking because I was able to consider it without attaching emotions or judgments. I was able to simply "sit with" the ideas and contemplate them. What I didn't realize was this shift was the beginning of a habit change. Plain and simple, I was changing from my previous habit to a new habit and way of thinking.

Perhaps the catalyst for this shift in thinking was feeling bored from doing the same kinds of physical activities that didn't challenge me fully. I wanted more in other areas of my life, as well: job position, money, travel, marriage, etc. But I didn't see any connection between the shift in thinking about those areas and taking on a new physical challenge. Instead, in my typical fashion, I waited for circumstances to change rather than being proactive about going beyond the edge of my comfort zone.

These same thoughts occurred to me when I read Born to Run (Christopher McDougall), about the Tarahumara people, who are American Indians isolated by the Copper Canyons of the Sierra Madre region in Mexico. These people have the ability to run hundreds of miles without resting or injuring themselves. McDougall also describes other top runners in the book. I came face to face with this kind of extraordinary running ability at the Leadville 100 event. Even after I did 13 miles of pacing a runner who I took across the finish line, I still wondered how they did it. The difference this time was that I wanted to know for myself. That led me to consider… If exceptional runners could do the Leadville 100, maybe I could do the Ironman.

I am an accomplisher. I am accustomed to completing anything I set my mind to—and doing it quickly! This translates into the expectation that I should be able to take on anything new and pick it up quickly. Reality slap: I learned in yoga I might not be good immediately at something that was new to me. A friend invited me to go with her to the first class. I felt awful and awkward, like a fish out of water. I had no idea what to do and couldn't do any of the moves or poses. Because she and I weren't very close friends, I acted polite and said, "Okay," when she asked me how I liked the class. Inside, I was mad! I vowed never to go back after we left. Then, my inner voice kept nagging at me: Why is yoga so good for people? How can they do it, and why can't I? It was the same thing I had learned in the Pikes Peak Ascent: I gave myself permission to continue thinking of how others did it, and then asked myself, How could I do that?

Thank goodness my friend asked me to go back to yoga three more times. Because of the sheer competitiveness I felt with her and within myself, I went. Yoga remained very difficult for me, but I saw people who could do things I couldn't. People seemed happy, healthy and well balanced from their yoga practice. I wanted that for me. Only then could I see a possible path to getting better, a possible path to figuring it out for myself. The key was to think of the first thing to do to figure it out—instead of being overwhelmed by trying to understand all of it. Feeling overwhelmed would have stopped me from doing anything. After I took the first step, I took another, and then another, and so on. Ultimately, taking these steps one at a time led me to completing a yogi training intensive program, which was the tipping point for my yoga.

This experience showed me it was a blessing that I wasn't good at yoga in the first class—or the second or third class. Having success or calling it quits at "good enough" weren't taking me further in making the strides that would bring me the change I wanted—in yoga or in other areas of my life. Ah-ha!

I learned, too, that regularly spending my free time with complacent people did not serve me well. People who didn't want to expand their comfort zone tended to encourage me to stay in the same place. It was more helpful to me to be around people who thought way bigger than I did—even if it scared me.

I wondered why we, as a society, feared the discomfort that comes from stretching our comfort zones? Is it cultural? Is it programming? I began to explore these questions and more as I began stretching my own comfort zones in my pursuit of competing in the Ironman World Championship in Kona, HI.

I learned what it took to tap into a dream and do all that was necessary to make it come true. In the process, I developed *The Seven Keys to Greater Success in Your Personal and Professional Life*. With these in hand, I have chosen to coach people in learning to embrace those moments when they are about to have a breakthrough and stretch their comfort zones. I believe it should be joyful to know that all we have to deal with is a little short-term, short-lived pain. Too often, we run and hide from these breakthrough moments and end up keeping our potential locked away.

Let's celebrate the human journey and honor our privilege to reach our true potential.

Chapter 1

A Personal Journey

I learned that personal journeys can be difficult to navigate, even if they are journeys you really want.

In February 2012, I moved out of the home I had shared with my husband, Allan. As a result of my training for the Ironman World Championship (the IM-WC) in Kona, Hawaii, I went from being focused to being ultra-focused. Part of gaining that focus was clarity and the painful realization that my husband and I did not share compatible dreams for our lives. In fact, he had tried to dissuade me from pursuing my dream for Kona.

Allan peppered me with questions. I dealt with storms of emotional emails from him during our separation. He wanted to know how to make our marriage work and whether we should divorce. He wanted answers about our future, so we decided to go to couples therapy.

When we agreed to go to therapy, I doubted he would be open to changing. It seemed to me he would simply want me to change. In therapy, he said he wanted the therapist to agree with him and tell me to change. I felt as if I were peeling off my skin, exposing emotional and spiritual nerve endings, but we never got anywhere. We just re-hashed all the same issues that got us there in the first place. I sat and cried while he blamed me for the failure of our marriage.

It gradually dawned on me that I had been increasingly angry over the previous year that Allan was unwilling to stretch his comfort zone or support me while I stretched mine. Once I realized this, the healing process began. My anger dissipated until I didn't have any left in me.

At the end of our counseling, the therapist told us we were stuck at an impasse. Unless we changed, life would stay the same. The thing was, I had already changed. My husband had made it clear: he did not want to be a part of the changes I was making in my life. I had moved out the previous month to pursue my goals for Kona. As with many marriages, this was not a clear-cut matter of right or wrong. It was simply two people arriving at the painful conclusion that they held different ideas about their journeys. I knew I needed to move on.

When Allan and I met, we had felt ideally suited. We had lots in common. We both loved working out and made it a priority in our lives. We had even gone to the same gym for two years. We loved Moab and Fruita and had ridden many of the same mountain bike trails. We each had been married once before. Ours had been a whirlwind courtship, and we had both felt ready to get married again.

Despite our many common interests and values, we could not resolve our differences. As often happens in a marriage, one partner became comfortable with keeping life going on an even keel while the other was comfortable embracing change. This is what happened with us.

While this marriage disruption was going on, I was transitioning into a new job as CEO of a real estate office that was struggling. My mission was to make it successful again, and there was lots of pressure to perform quickly. The office had a staff of four and 70 real estate agents—all of whom I had to get to know in the first 30 days while recruiting new ones, teaching classes, assessing staff, and establishing a vision.

It was a challenge to manage my career and pursue Kona. Preparation went beyond the training schedule. It included seeing a massage therapist, appointments with chiropractors, getting equipment, and keeping up with nutrition. It was a big learning curve for me, especially since this was the biggest challenge in my life to date.

Business problems compounded the "busy-ness" of my Kona preparation. There were people who seemed to be sucking the energy out of me—including a secretary who got pay increases but didn't fulfill the basic duties of the position. It seemed no one wanted to be proactive about this problem. I decided to let her go, and she filed an employment complaint afterward. The subsequent entangled legalities intensified my stress.

I had previously purchased ownership in another Keller Williams real estate franchise office where I had been a top agent. That made me a candidate for leadership. Yet, when I stepped into the leadership role at my new office, my co-owners who had once felt like my family forced me to sell my interest. It was devastating, and I wasn't sure how to go forward. I chose to sell rather than fight it, sparing myself the energy and pain. Then I ran into another problem. I had purchased the shares from a retirement account. I found out that the taxes hadn't been filed properly and there were penalties in the amount of $20,000. During our marriage my husband and I had co-mingled our funds, yet at this point he decided it was my bill and tried to get the IRS to go after me alone for the payment. Needless to say, the amount of stress I was under was crushing.

While I was dealing with these struggles, I was training a few hours a day and going to races. Some days, it felt like the odds were against me and I was being pushed down. I was always sleep-deprived. Deep inside my soul, I believed the obstacles cropping up were because of my decision to pursue my goal and that they were a part of my challenge and a necessary component on my path to achieving what I wanted.

There were a million things I needed to accomplish each day, and I was always surrounded by reminders to call people back. There were a multitude of challenges to which I had to rise, and in my training, my list of what to prepare was getting longer. Sleep, rest, work, and socializing were all getting short shrift. I almost always had another conversation playing somewhere in the back of my head. I could never fully concentrate on what was happening in front of me. I knew that if anything got off track, I would feel buried. The weekends were never a saving grace. I would do an especially long bike ride, 50 to 90 miles, and run

1.5 to 4 hours, with weight training after each. I was physically, emotionally and mentally drained by the time I was done.

From this inner and outer turmoil, I discovered that no matter how many struggles I encountered in my personal and professional life, my training remained the constant. If I was consistent with it, I could always count on it. During training, I pushed all of the other busy-ness off to the side and concentrated on what I was doing and where I was headed. I kept my vision clear. I focused on my main goal, and I just let the chaos and busy-ness be. This had been difficult for me in the past, and I would become overwhelmed. By the time I was in full pursuit of my Kona dream, I had learned that being focused on several big goals chunked down into small, step-by-step pieces, helped me alleviate the overwhelm and let me perform. I couldn't let anything else get in the way and didn't allow myself to make excuses. I also found that by focusing on my training and completing it well, I was able to focus on the business or personal side of my life in an all-in fashion, which enabled me to do better in all of the areas.

Training for Kona taught me how to separate life's daily obligations from profound personal goals. I learned how to be driven and to believe in my purpose. Key to this was reminding myself that the struggles were temporary— they wouldn't be there forever. Even though frustration and anger came up, I was able to learn a quiet patience and keep going. There were days I couldn't be bothered to think past the fourth or fifth item on my to-do lists. Then, all of a sudden, a steady perseverance of spirit appeared to steady and fortify me as I trained. And my spiritual journey had begun...

TAP INTO THE DREAM/FEEL THE DREAM, ASK FOR HELP, & HAVE FAITH

Chapter 2

The Fascination of Ironman

In 1982 when Julie Moss participated in the Ironman race, her motive was to gather research for her physiology thesis for her degree. As Moss neared the end of the race, fatigue and dehydration set in. She fell only yards away from the finish line, and another athlete passed her to claim the women's title. Moss did not give up. She actually crawled across the finish line—dragging her body along the ground. Her strength in those last few moments created a mantra that has endured: just finishing the Ironman is a victory in itself.

When I watched Julie Moss' performance on television, I was mesmerized. I couldn't tear my eyes away from the screen. Her race was horrifying and incredible all at the same time. I wondered how she could drag herself along to finish the race, why she did it, and where she found the strength. I didn't understand it at all. A few days later, I watched her being interviewed on "Good Morning America," and she was beaming with confidence.

Every year after that, I got together with my sister, Ruby, to watch the Ironman competition. And each year, we would cry as the people were stretched to their limits—physically and mentally—in the contest. So few people could complete the race that it seemed like the quintessential test of a person's will.

Ruby is a remarkable person, and she is one of the biggest supporters of me in every aspect of my life. She was not surprised when I told her I was going to train to compete in the Ironman. After our many years of watching the World Championships together, it probably seemed only natural to her, and she was right there to believe in me and support me in whatever it was going to take to get me there.

What exactly is the Ironman? It is a triathlon, a series of races organized by the World Triathlon Corporation. It consists of a 2.4-mile swim, a 112-mile bicycle ride, and a 26.2-mile run. It is all raced without a break. Each Ironman event has a time cutoff to meet. The swim starts at 7 a.m. and needs to be done within 2 hours and 20 minutes. The bike ride cut off is 5:30 p.m., and the entire triathlon must be completed by midnight.

The Ironman Triathlon was founded after top runners and swimmers in the 1977 Oahu Perimeter Relay debated at the awards ceremonies about which type of athlete was the most fit. United States Navy Commander, John Collins, who was also an athlete, suggested the debate be settled by combining all three of the long-distance competitions already established in Hawaii. These were the Waikiki Roughwater Swim, the Around Oahu Bike Race, and the Honolulu Marathon. He was so inspired by the idea that he went to the stage and issued the challenge, saying that whoever got to the finish line first would be aptly dubbed "the Ironman."

Commander Collins made plans for how the course would run, including the swimming and bike legs of the race. Before the race started, each athlete was given instructions for each portion of the triathlon. The athletes were told that completing the race would give them "bragging rights for life", which is now part of the Ironman trademark.

During the event, each of the athletes had their own crew to provide water, food, and emotional support. The first race began on February 18, 1978, and of the fifteen men who participated that first year, twelve completed the race. Gordon Haller was the first person to earn the title of "Ironman."

Held in Hawaii every year since then, the Ironman Triathlon has become known worldwide for its grueling length and harsh conditions. It is one of the ultimate tests of strength and endurance.

The Ironman Triathlon has expanded since its 1978 inception. The following year—with no marketing and simply by word-of-mouth—the race attracted 50 athletes. Tom Warren became the 1979 Ironman and Lyn Lemaire, who finished in sixth place, became the first "Ironwoman."

Sports Illustrated writer Barry McDermott, in Hawaii for a golf tournament, heard of the race and wrote a ten-page account of Ironman. Coverage by Sports Illustrated and the "ABC Wide World of Sports" drew more attention to the Ironman competition. Within a few years, the number of athletes applying to participate went from dozens, to hundreds, to thousands. Because of the increased interest, the Ironman was moved to a less-urbanized part of the island. The move to the heat and wind of Kona from Oahu also made the Ironman event more difficult. The Ironman Triathlon continued to grow in popularity, and in 1994 the Olympic Committee added the triathlon as a medal event.

The Kona IM-WC is an endurance race held in grueling conditions. Certain wet suits are not even allowed during the Ironman because they are too buoyant. The swim in the Kailua Bay is subject to big waves, choppy water, and sea life. The cycling hills have moderate grades and strong crosswinds that have been known to knock riders down to the ground. To round it out, athletes face strong winds and hot temperatures during the running leg of the course.

To date, the Ironman remains unaltered and the Hawaiian Ironman World Championship in Kona is regarded as the most well-honored and prestigious triathlon worldwide. Although thousands of athletes participate in Ironman events to improve times or set records, a limited number of spots exist for Kona. Just finishing the Ironman is a high point in the careers of many triathletes. The annual race in Hawaii has become known as the Ironman World Championship and includes a swim in the bay off Kailua-Kona, a biking leg through the Hawaiian lava desert and back, and a marathon along the coast. This is widely touted as one of the hardest races in the world, and I was taking it on because I had always dreamed of doing it.

There are 28 Ironman triathlon races around the world to qualify contestants for the Ironman World Championship in Kona. Professional athletes qualify via a point system based on their performance at Ironman events. Amateur athletes may qualify for a limited number of slots allocated for different age groups. Each of the Ironman races has its own set of tests of physical and emotional endurance. The Kona Ironman makes other events pale in comparison and thus possesses a certain mystique for all triathletes.

There are 2,000 slots for the Ironman World Championship (IM WC), and there are 90,000 people competing for those slots every year. There are three slots for each age group for each qualifying race. You need a 1st, 2nd or 3rd place in each competition of a race to get a slot. You have to be fast!

In May through June 2010, I took a real estate and life training program offered through Keller Williams. A wonderful man named John Prescott who was a top real estate agent in the country and a man of great faith taught the course. He taught me what limiting beliefs are and how the brain processes information—and, in turn, how this influences us to accomplish goals or shy away from them in fear. John challenged and empowered me to stretch my comfort zone in business. This translated into my personal life in a big way. My business changed during the six-week class. I did things I never thought I was capable of; I ended up going door-to-door in our neighborhood to talk about the real estate business. My husband thought I was crazy. In my personal life, I kept thinking of what was next. My faith in my potential began to grow.

During the class, we did an exercise where we wrote down our dreams. I wrote down "Kona – IM WC" before I even realized it—it was an immediate, gut-level honest answer. This exercise stuck with me because it drove home how important this dream was to me. I was out to experience the feeling of having this dream become reality.

Chapter 3

First Inklings of Kona

The Leadville Trail 100 Run started in 1983 with just 45 runners. It is an ultramarathon held annually on trails and dirt roads near Leadville, Colorado, through the heart of the Rocky Mountains. Participants climb and descend 15,600 feet, with elevations ranging between 9,200 and 12,620 feet.

In Born to Run, Christopher McDougall calls the Leadville 100 one of the ultimate endurance tests. The chance to participate in this race surprisingly presented itself to me in August of 2010. I was excited to share McDougall's book with a friend who was an ultra-runner, that is, a runner who competes at distances longer than the marathon 26.2 miles. After I shared it with him, he told me about an opportunity to not only pace two brothers who were running the Leadville 100, but also to see other athletes who inspired me from the book.

Pacing a runner can be as simple as keeping them company and letting them hit their paces. But if you really are there to "pace" them, you help by serving them. You might be their voice of reason and reality check to help them remember not to run too fast in their early miles, for example. You may also serve by carrying their extra nutrition and fluids or to get water for them at designated water stops. Pacing can be tricky. To truly serve the other person's needs, you need to know his or her likes and dislikes. I was hesitant to pace at first, insisting I was not a fast runner and felt I had no business pacing another runner. He was quick to point out that we couldn't even start pacing our runner until mile 50, so he wouldn't be running fast.

I took some time to think about it, and he continued to encourage me to do it. Finally, I said yes and got excited about the particulars and the race. As the details were firmed up, I received an email listing the pace-runners and legs assigned. I was stunned to find that I had been awarded the final 13 miles of the race, which meant I would be taking the runner across the finish line. I couldn't fathom why they were giving it to me, but they insisted that I was well suited for it. I thought for sure everyone else on the team was better than me. This is something that people run into when they are getting closer to creating their dream: a resistance to embrace your own passion and someone else's recognition that you have what it takes to achieve that dream. Ultimately, I figured it would be an amazing experience, and I should take it in and learn all that I could.

What I saw blew me away and was more powerful than anything I could have imagined. I saw the indomitable spirit and iron will of the participants, especially the runner who I paced, Brad. Since my turn was last, I got to see all of the other pacers get ready. Then I went to bed and was able to get a few short hours of sleep before I picked the runner up at 2 a.m. During my short nap, I woke up to a ringing cell phone. Brad's dad was on the line, explaining that our runner had encountered stomach problems, slowed down, and crawled into the car to sleep for one hour. I was suddenly worried that he might not make it, but his dad said to show up an hour later at the checkpoint. Brad had completed this race three times before, as well as others more grueling, so the chances were good he would pull through.

My husband Allan was with me at the race. We had a challenge driving to each aid station at approximately every 13 or more miles, depending upon the terrain through the wilderness. Sometimes the station was a big tent. Other times, it was just a table and a volunteer to record that the runner had been there—

leaving competitors' crews the job of providing all the provisions, including a chair to sit down on if the runner wanted to change shoes or socks or put on or remove gear at the top or bottom of a big mountain pass. And since this race is continuous, the crews waited in the middle of the night for their runner with only headlamps and flashlights. After mile 50, pacers could start with their runner, and so every pacing leg I would watch the next pacer put on their water pack, socks, shoes, hat, protective clothing, their nutrition and that of their runner, and start the process of running with and keeping their competitor on time and lucid. Every time I watched this process, I got butterflies. I was hoping to take in every shred of information that would be helpful for my leg. All the while, I felt like an imposter. Even though I had been a life-long athlete, I had never done anything like this. I had only read a book about it and didn't think that necessarily qualified me to be there. I felt at any moment someone would say, "Hey, you shouldn't be here. What have you done to prove you should be here?" That can be what it is like when a dream is coming into focus for you. You can see everything in you that is not in line with the dream.

At 3:30 a.m., I was at the checkpoint in the motionless night. The stillness was broken only by the small runner's aid station and the headlamps of racers passing through it. It was freezing cold and we huddled around the only heater in the area, waiting for Brad. At this point, I went to use the bathroom, a port-o-let out in the open at the top of a clearing by the aid station. I had no sooner gotten there that my husband was outside, pounding on the door. Brad had just come in and already left the aid station, and I needed to hurry and catch him! I couldn't believe my ears! I took off as fast as I could with my headlamp on, running through the darkness.

A steady stream of thoughts cascaded through my mind: Wait a minute, how did he get by me so fast? How did he sleep in his car with stomach problems and then wake himself up and force himself back out into the cold and start running again? How did he gain the speed to fly through the aid station at mile 87? I was flabbergasted and worried that my chance to help him, understand how he did it, and what drove him was disintegrating. I was running on a trail through the woods as fast as I could, nervous about injuring myself, with only a headlamp and the moon lighting the way.

When I caught up to Brad, his dad was running at a decent pace with him. They walked every few minutes, all carefully choreographed to keep him on track to finish by the 29-hour cutoff. Dan handed me the stuff I needed to carry: a bottle of water and a baggie of Chex Mix—all he was currently able to keep down. I was dumbstruck. I must have stood there for too long because the runner said, "Alright, let's go already."

While I had the opportunity, I spoke with him and heard more about his story and training. The conversation was punctuated by him consistently checking a "schedule," which was a slender printed piece stuck to his forearm listing the markers and the times needed at each to ensure finishing the race by the deadline. We would walk for a bit and then he would look at it and say, "Okay, time to run," and would tell me to time us for a specific period until we got to the next landmark on the course.

I asked Brad how he had completed the Leadville 100 and other tougher races so many times. He explained that he did it to prove to himself that he could. Sometimes he took more training time than others—but in doing something that many others found impossible, he had found something he loved. He also loved showing his sons that they could do anything they wanted if they put their minds to it. He said that proving to himself that he could do these things translated into all of the other parts of his life. He applied that inspiration, passion, and belief in himself and his abilities to the other challenges before him—and it made all the difference. He also said it kept him in shape!

Finally, we were at the finish line. As the sun came up, Brad put on his American flag bandana, and he and his kids crossed the finish line together, crying. It's an unwritten, yet well-heeded rule that pacers don't cross the finish line with their runner. This was explained to me before I started my pacing stint and it made sense. So, as his wife and kids came alongside him as we closed in on the finish, I slowly peeled off to the side and watched him cross. It was honorable and humble to do so. With that, I started to cry, realizing what I had just witnessed. Such a monumental accomplishment, and I had gotten to hear his thoughts along the way and be part of his experience and success. I felt pride in him and a deep sense of humility as I compared myself to him.

Brad inspired me, and I saw something in myself that I had never before seen: I was the only one holding me back. I asked myself what I had to lose in pursuing Kona. I began tapping into my dream.

Once the race finished, Allan and I went back to Dan's house where we were staying. There were about 20 people staying in this very small, old mining house. When we arrived, most were either still in town, on the course, around the finish, or had gone home. One athlete was there who had been dubbed a "Leadman" because he had officially completed a Leadville Trail Marathon, the Silver Rush 50 MTB or Run, then moved on to the Leadville Trail 100 MTB, 10K run, and finally the legendary Leadville Trail 100 Run, all within six weeks. They award every Leadville 100 footrace or mountain bike race finisher a belt buckle, and the Leadman and Leadwoman get bigger ones.

As we sat in the kitchen, congratulating him on this even more monumental accomplishment, he was blending up a recovery drink and trying to eat. Several things struck me during this conversation. He was shuffling his feet to move around, no longer able to pick them up. His eyes were completely bloodshot, and when he looked at you, it was with an empty gaze. He wasn't really making sense when he talked. His sense of time was distorted and he was confusing events that had happened. I had never seen this before and started to correct him, but Allan stopped me. Later, he explained that this is what it looks like when you push yourself to and beyond your physical and mental limits. It was scary to me, and stuck with me for a long time afterwards. I can still see his face, like it was yesterday. And it seemed like he did it all for a bigger belt buckle. Or maybe he did it because this was his dream.

Chapter 4

Utah Triathlon Festival

There were events that sharpened my resolve and strengthened me in body, mind, and spirit. The year was 2011, and it began with the Utah Triathlon Festival in Moab in May.

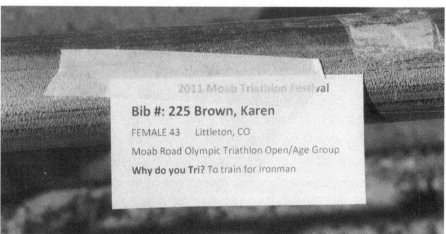

Utah Triathlon Race Marker

I set out to Moab for an Olympic distance triathlon. Olympic distance meant a 0.93-mile swim, a 24.8-mile bike ride, and a 6.2-mile run. I had been in Moab to mountain bike before. I enjoyed returning to a familiar place. I knew it would offer me a sense of comfort and belonging—feelings I wouldn't derive from other races

I was still married at this point, and since my husband and I knew the area, we decided to go two days early and stay a day after the race to go mountain biking on some of our favorite trails. When we arrived in Moab, we went right to the state park where the race was to be held. Other triathletes were already there, running, biking, and swimming. Even though it was nothing like the sheer number of athletes that would descend on Kona for the IM WC, it was still initially overwhelming and intimidating to see so many athletes already preparing.

The first person I met was a woman from Colorado who was also racing. Talking with her helped calm my nerves. My stomach churned as I thought about all the details of the race and how the swim would go. Swimming was not my strong suit by far—my swim stroke wasn't efficient, and it was troubling me. I was using the workouts given to me by my coach, along with an occasional swim lesson. I didn't feel I was progressing, but I pressed on and recommitted to training harder. I prayed that it would click one day.

Before the trip, I decided to purchase a professional-level wet suit. I was trying the suit for the first time when I prepared to practice in the lake where we would race. Nervousness seeped in as I put the suit on. I worried it would not provide enough insulation and I would get too cold during the race. My coach and other triathletes had shared stories of becoming hypothermic during their races. I didn't like swimming in cold water, so I placed a neoprene cap over my regular swim cap. I decided to use full booties and gloves for my feet and hands, so I could be warm from head to toe. The practice swim went okay, and I didn't get too cold with all of my gear on. However, I was still nervous.

I also felt shaky on my new tri bike because I had not yet raced on it. There was so much running through my head—race details, the pre-race and race day prep, hydration and nutrition. My mind felt clouded.

Before I left for Moab, my coach told me to set up my drinking water bottle on the bike with a straw and sponge to block water from spilling and prevent dirt from getting in. We went over how long the race would last and where the aid stations were, in case it was a scorching day and I needed more water. We discussed having energy gels in transition (the areas where the legs of the race change from swimming to biking to running) and when to ingest them. Energy gels come in single-serve packets and are normally used for endurance events like triathlons, running, and cycling events. The carbohydrates in the gels are absorbed by the blood and supply the body with calories and nutrients to reduce muscle fatigue, raise blood sugar, and enhance performance. Energy gels normally don't have fat, fiber, or protein, so the body can digest them more quickly. They are supposed to be used 15 minutes before starting an event and then hourly after the first 60 minutes of the race. I had to make sure I consumed the gels with water so I wouldn't become dehydrated and have an upset stomach, as many triathletes had experienced.

During the practice ride, I wore a slender pack on my back for water, not wanting to put my race bottle on until race day. I rode several parts of the somewhat bumpy course, and the bike felt good. I started to plan ahead, thinking of where I would have gels and water along the way. The running course was on trails. Even though it was a bit long, I was comfortable with the prospect of running this course since I had loved trail running in Colorado.

One of my biggest worries was wearing the race kit shorts and top under my wet suit and being cold and wet when I got onto the bike for the next segment of the race. A race kit is a pair of matching biking shorts and tank top that are breathable and made of thin material. It's just so comfortable and light, you don't think about it during the race.

I hadn't thought about having to solve any problems and hadn't come up with contingencies. A problem I didn't expect was that the road surface was a rough chip seal that resembled aggregate. The ride was bumpy and I worried that the skinny tires on my bike wouldn't hold up. Most of the triathletes in the race were going to be on the Xterra (off-road) portion of the pavement and had mountain bikes. I was in the minority of triathletes on road bikes; accommodating us seemed like an afterthought.

When we went to the transition area of the race to see where my bike and gear would go, we saw a sticker with my name on it. I was overwhelmed with a sense of pride and excitement, and my husband took a picture of it (see page 29).

As with every race, a pre-race meeting was held for the athletes to go over the course and the activities of the race the next day. They went over what time the transition area would open in the morning, covered how no other athletes were allowed, and explained where the buoys would be placed for the swimming leg.

The night before the race, I got excited when I was body marked—event identification information listed on our skin in waterproof marker—because I realized I was officially in triathlon racing. The information included age group and participation numbers that let officials and photographers more easily identify you. Many times that night, I glanced down at my black numbers and thought about the race. I reminded myself this race was the first step toward racing in Kona.

Swimmers in Lake

The first leg—swimming—was tough. It took forever. I couldn't swim straight and missed the buoy, requiring me to go back and go around it the right way. Even though it was less than a mile, I was dizzy when I got out of the water. My balance was off and I had a hard time peeling off my wet suit despite having practiced it. When I reached transition, my bike was the only one left on the racks. I kept going, put my shoes and helmet on, and was still feeling disoriented.

As I ran to the end of the transition area, I got off balance and fell down with my bike, at which time my water spilled out of my race bottle. I didn't see that it had emptied until I was on the course. When I realized it, I knew what contingency to prepare for in future races.

There weren't water stations on the course since it was "only" 25 miles. I didn't have any idea what I was going to do, but I calmed myself and kept going. The course was pretty straightforward and there weren't many road cyclists since the draw of this race was the Xterra trail. (Xterra is a triathlon with the cycling portion on mountain bikes and terrain.) The road bikers killed me in the swim and were already long gone from transition when I got there. I had gels with me, but knew it was only a matter of time before I needed water. This was a "short" race, so I was pushing the speed and really working.

About two-thirds of the way through the bike leg, I came to the uphill: a solid incline for eight miles. I happen to love hills and see them as the fun part, so I excelled. Still, I was concerned about putting out too much and hitting the wall. My comforting thought was that at the end of an uphill is a downhill, and I could save energy and fly back to the transition to make up some of the time that I lost during the swim.

My plan almost worked. At the end of the first downhill section, I came across a sheriff who was directing traffic. I begged him for something to drink and he generously gave me his unopened bottle of Gatorade. I drank it down in one continuous stream and thanked him profusely. I turned to finish the downhill and the end of the bike leg and was going along fast and smooth when I heard a "BAM!" followed by a hissing sound. I quickly looked at both tires and saw my back tire was flat. I slowed down, stopped, dismounted and took the wheel off to fix the flat. I knew I had a spare tube with me. I only worried about the time it would take to change it.

As I pulled out the spare and compared it to the flat one, I noticed that the stems were different lengths. Another contingency learned! I had put on race wheels with deep walls, so the stem was extra-long to get through the wall. My replacement tube had a standard stem, which meant it would be too short. I thought, Well, I'm sunk. My race is over. Then I remembered that I had another spare tube in my bike bag in the car back at the transition area. I had to figure out how to get to it or get someone to bring it to me. I thought of the sheriff. He was sweeping the last cyclists through the course, which meant he would be coming by me and might let me use his cell phone. The sheriff showed up and he let me use his cell phone to call my husband Allan to get the tube to me.

While I waited for him, I realized that I could pick up my bike and walk with it over my shoulder, carrying my wheel. I desperately wanted not to lose all that time just sitting on the side of the road. Thankfully, my husband had ridden with me on the practice ride, so he knew where I would be. I had walked quite a ways when he showed up with the bike bag. I switched out the tube, put the wheel back on and rode to the finish.

I returned to the transition area and racked my bike, changed my shoes and hat, and headed out for the run. This was my favorite part of the race! The run consisted of two loops on a trail, over a river and rocks, and then down a gravel road to the finish. The good news was there were two water stations on the course!

Switching from cycling to running can produce significant muscle weakness and thigh pain that can slow you down considerably. To avert this, triathletes train by doing workouts known as "bricks": back-to-back workouts involving cycling and running. I had practiced a few bricks so my legs didn't feel completely brick-like in this running portion, but it did take some time to get going and feel comfortable in my stride.

Both loops went without incident but certainly weren't fast. I was so far behind everyone else that I was virtually by myself on the run. I didn't focus on that, however. I concentrated on the experience and what I was learning from it. I felt like those experiences were making me better so I could get to Kona.

After I finished, we collected my gear and took things back to the car. I was happy and relieved to have this race under my belt, and, though it didn't go smoothly at all, I thought, These are the kinds of things I need to learn to get to my goal of the Kona IM WC.

I was putting everything away and changing my clothes when I heard, "Karen Brown from Littleton, Colorado." I asked my husband if he had heard it, too, and he said yes. We realized they were giving away medals and prizes and had called my name. I said, "Maybe there's a medal for the slowest competitor and they're giving it to me!" We made our way back to the finish line where they had set up wooden podiums as well as a table with medals and lots of gift cards and swag. I asked the announcer if he had called my name. He looked on his clipboard and said that I had earned second place in my age group, women age 40-45.

He put a medal with a red ribbon around my neck. I was shocked! My times for this race were: swim, 44:15; bike, 2:05:54; run, 1:14:01; total time of 4:13:53. There were only three people in my age group and two finished. The competitor who would have gotten third place hadn't finished, but I didn't care. I was giddy that I got anything at all, especially with everything that had gone wrong. I asked my husband to take a photo of me on the podium to commemorate the experience. Sometimes, you just have to laugh at yourself and enjoy the funny things that happen.

Chapter 5

My Formative Years

I was born prematurely, and my parents were told I might not make it. Even as a newborn, I showed I could triumph over difficulty! I proved to the doctor that not only would I make it, I would thrive.

My mom and dad had been childhood sweethearts. Yet, my dad was not faithful to my mom, and he had cheated on her (again) while she was pregnant with me. Like any mother wanting a stable environment for her children, she tried to work things out with him and thought she had, only to find all he had done was lie to her. She went through the rest of her pregnancy, depressed, hopeless, and barely eating. She was highly stressed by the impossible choice of being a single mom, with a husband or without one, and she wasn't gaining the weight she should have

Karen as a baby

been. As a result, she delivered me early. I was to be born in March and came in late January. After I was born, she decided she had to leave my dad for all of us to have a better life. She packed up my sister and me when I was three months old, along with everything we could fit in the car. We left in the evening when my dad had gone out to carouse. I was too little to remember it, but my sister remembers. She said she was terrified and sad because she had idolized my dad. My mom tried to help her cope by telling her we were going to go stay with Grandma, and she could see her dad anytime she wanted. We stayed with my maternal grandmother after whom Ruby was named. She watched us during the day while my mom—then only 24—worked as a secretary. My family of aunts, uncles and cousins were supportive of my mom and us, too. It was 1968, and the prospects for a single woman to earn a solid living on which to raise two babies were slim to non-existent.

Our father had already started a new family with the woman with whom he had been having the affair. Ruby and I did not have much to do with him after our parents split, and I really did not have a connection with my dad.

My mother was a true example of an independent woman. She worked her way up to better-paying jobs, and she always said I didn't need anyone else to support me and not to let anyone tell me differently.

Mom eventually remarried when I was four years old, and we got along well with my step-dad. He was a good father figure to my sister and me. He came to watch us play sports and even helped coach a couple of our teams. He fostered our goals and dreams. My step-dad ended up legally adopting us, so we took on his name. We were a family, happy for 13 years or so, while Ruby and I grew into young women and my mom and step-dad climbed corporate ladders, making a nice life for us. On Mother's Day when I was 17 years old, my step-dad asked my mom for a divorce. Later, she found out he had most likely been cheating. They divorced and, because I felt he had betrayed my mom with his infidelity, I decided not to have anything further to do with him. Looking back, I think my mom settled in her choice of men because she was tired of doing it all and tired of looking for someone. I saw this, and it rubbed off on me, unfortunately.

My sister, Ruby has always been an integral part of my life. Growing up, she was always at my service. I would scream and cry until Ruby fetched things for me. She did everything for me, so much so that it got to the point that my mom needed to prevent her from helping me so I could learn how to speak and do things on my own!

My mom continued to be a driving force in my life, as she always led by example and offered encouragement—assuring me I could do anything I wanted in life. She said there was always a way to reach my goals. When I was growing up, Mom often gave me more responsibility than I could handle. That in turn made me want more, and I became very driven to attain any goals I set for myself. My mother was an achiever. There were times she struggled with depression, yet I saw her keep going and keep her head up. She would not let anyone stand in her way. My mom always told me I was special and her repetition of this statement made me believe it. I would hold on to all of this as I pursued my dreams in life.

When we lived in Colorado Springs for four years, we had a babysitter named Margie. At her house, her teenage son frequently backed me into the wall between two bunk beds and beat me with a belt. I would get so scared I would wet my pants. I didn't say anything to my mom or my sister. Despite the bruises on my arms, I would act like I was just playing rough. I continued to have bruises for three months until one day my mom noticed that my dress was wet and put two and two together. From that day on, we never went to Margie's house again. However, the damage to my psyche was done. From then on, I was terrified of men who spoke very loud or aggressively because they reminded me of my abuser.

My sister was beside herself when she found out what happened at the babysitter's. Ruby was always there to protect me and look out for me. I think she felt guilty that she hadn't kept me out of harm's way, even though she was just a child and she hadn't known about it.

I carried this abuse with me for a long time—especially in work relationships with men who were challenging or authoritative. The way that they spoke, the pitch of their voice—the fear of wetting myself again—would all resurface. My memories would take me back to feeling like a little kid with a threatening bigger kid towering over me. Even though in every other aspect of my life, I was very strong, driven and sure of myself, I felt like I needed to act out, retaliate, or lie down and cry around authoritative men. I would wilt like a flower around them.

The scars of abuse eventually manifested themselves in my believing that I was not good enough. I had internalized a belief that life held good things in store for other people, but not for me. I had the two most common consequences of childhood abuse: damaged self-worth and lack of healthy self-acceptance.

It took its toll. The good news is there is strength gained from trauma. I went to therapy several times in my life. As I matured, I was able to identify the triggers that led to my feelings of inadequacy and low self-worth. I could then change my reactions and heal. I ended up with more inner drive and resolve to overcome whatever obstacles I faced.

In some ways, the abandonment by my father carried over into my marriages more than did the abuse. I looked for and twice found husbands who were financially stable but emotionally unavailable. Even though they were not good matches for me, I was attracted to their stability, their consistency, and their loyalty. This epiphany came to me after my second marriage. I had thought camaraderie and shared interests would be enough to create a strong partnership. It turns out I need much more in a life partner. I don't relate deeply to men who don't deal well with discussing fears and feelings. I've come to realize being able to interpret the world through a variety of emotions, dreams, and goals is paramount to me. I'm not comfortable with black-and-white, right-or-wrong types of thinking and can't confine myself to small thinkers with fixed mindsets.

My first husband, Ian, from England was an example of a man who was emotionally unavailable. It's no surprise that I met him at the gym, and equally not surprising that our marriage lasted for less than a year. At 29 years old, I was very ready to get married and so was Ian, but our visions for a future together weren't in sync. He was looking for a traditional wife who wanted children and a home-life. I was a total career person. I didn't want kids, and he did, but he wasn't being honest with himself or me about it. And, we happily went ahead with a big traditional wedding with twenty family and friends coming over from England.

Our marriage got off to a bad start right from our wedding day. He got so drunk at the reception that he passed out after getting sick at the hotel. I spent my wedding night sitting in my wedding dress on the bed watching the news about Princess Diana being killed in a car crash.

We had chosen to put off a honeymoon for a few months because our English guests were staying at our house for two weeks for the wedding. Shortly after they left for home, Ian changed completely. He started spending more time at work, less time with me and seemed to flat-out not want to be with me at all. When we did spend time together, he always had to have the same two or three couples around and spend most of that time laughing for hours with the wives, with whom he seemed to have a good connection. Finally, I confronted him and asked if he was having an affair with one of them. He slowly answered "no"…but he was on his way to having one. I was torn up emotionally and finally suggested marriage counseling. He was reluctant, and then I said I would go on my own to get some answers and relief for myself. Out of guilt, he said he would go, too. Our marriage counseling never worked—I cried all the time, and he kept saying, "I don't know, I don't know," in response to questions. We got nowhere. Finally, he went back to England for Christmas and New Year's and that year (1997), I realized it was over and I had to move on. We listed our house for sale on my birthday at the end of January and it was sold by Valentine's Day.

Though my relationships with men ended up being difficult after I grew up, I really had a good childhood with my mother and sister. I was blessed to have a good home life and a childhood filled with laughter and love. I enjoyed athletics and participated in baton twirling, gymnastics, biking, running, softball, volleyball, basketball, and tennis. At one point, I was one of only two girls who played on an all-boys basketball team! I had to prove myself to them by showing them I could play well and move fast.

As a teenager, I was on a girl's fast-pitch softball team, which was one of my favorite experiences. It wasn't just about the winning. The three coaches had been college buddies who proved to be great role models and who showed us we could work hard and have fun at the same time.

Karen on the basketball team

I've learned some of the greatest lessons in my life from playing sports—including what it means to never give up. I excelled, and sports would provide a safe haven for me for the rest of my life.

When I was in the seventh grade, my maternal grandmother Ruby died suddenly of an aneurysm. She and my grandpa were playing BINGO at the VFW hall, and she just slumped over and was gone. There was nothing the doctors could do. She was the epitome of everything a grandma should be—funny, loving and caring. You could tell that there was nothing and no one my grandpa loved more than her.

He was a gruff guy, older than she. He was a practical man, too. He had built a cabin in a very secluded, heavily wooded area with rutted dirt roads, and we would go there each summer. When I was twelve, my grandpa told me if something happened to them at the cabin there would be no way to get help since there wasn't a phone there. So, he insisted on teaching me how to drive. I was scared, but he sat next to me and talked me through it so I felt comfortable enough to drive in case of an emergency. Both my grandparents smoked, so maybe he knew something might eventually happen to them, and we would all need to be well prepared.

The last time we visited my grandparents at their house, I didn't want to leave. I wanted to stay with my grandmother. I just couldn't let her go. Eventually my mom calmed me down and got me into the car. Looking back, perhaps I sensed she was going to pass away soon.

My grandparents always taught me I could do anything. They believed in me. I have often thought back to them during difficult times to draw strength and courage. Even now, years later, I can hear them reminding me that my inner drive would always help me realize my dreams.

Years after my grandmother's passing, my mom had an ocular aneurysm, but they caught it early. Since Ruby and I know the propensity for aneurysm in our family, we are checked regularly and have an MRI every ten years. From this, I've come to appreciate that life is more fleeting than we realize and we need to act on our dreams while we can.

My family members have shown me what it means to pursue one's dreams. My great-aunt, Mary, was always go-getter and trailblazer; in the Navy as a young woman in the 1930's, she owned and operated her own horse ranch after competing in the equestrian community. She was at the top in a male-dominated arena. Aunt Mary did things unheard of for a woman. Having strong women like her in my life to look up to showed me I was the only one who would take care of me. I knew to focus on my pursuits, rather than give them up for someone else.

When I was fifteen years old, I was engrossed in fashion, and went after jobs in that arena. I worked at a well-known clothing store chain. My boss, Jenelle, was driven and accomplished, but she was also a hard-ass (aptly defined by the Random House Webster's Unabridged Dictionary as "a person who follows rules and regulations meticulously and enforces them without exception"). I knew that I wanted to progress to store manager eventually. Just before my 18th birthday, Jenelle sat me down to talk about what I had in mind after high school graduation. She wanted to make sure I was going to college. At that point, I had never really considered going to college and didn't think it was necessary. Jenelle told me there was no way she would promote me to a store manager position if I had never been to college. I was furious—if very naive—and left that job, but Janelle's words stuck with me.

After I graduated high school, I ended up going to college for a degree in fashion at Parks Junior College in north Denver. Each morning, I attended

school, and then went to a store management program in the afternoon. I worked at a women's clothing store until nine at night and then went home to study. When I was about 21, I was promoted to store manager for an upscale women's clothing store in downtown Denver. Boy, I thought I knew it all!

I look back now and see that I was spoiled during my mid-twenties. I worked full time and went to school full time, but I was messy and lived at home. When I graduated college, I moved out on my own and took on larger stores, but I

GOLDEN HIGH SCHOOL
Commencement
May 31, 1986

Karen's High School Graduation

wondered what was next. I was working for a privately owned company that only had three positions above my position as store manager. When I was passed over for a promotion, I was upset and started looking for a new job. I found an ad in the newspaper for someone to manage temporary leases in a shopping center in Colorado Springs. I knew nothing about leasing, but was so intrigued by the prospect that I applied for the job. I was among about 200 applicants, but I was ultimately given the job because of my retail experience. I ended up working for two of the best people I ever could have found, Steve and Dee. They shepherded me and showed me everything. I had to move back to Colorado Springs for the position, but since I knew the area and my extended family lived there, the prospect brought excitement rather than fear. I worked at this job for three or four years and became friends with a coworker, Glenn—a friendship that has grown and deepened over some 20-plus years, even after he moved to Kansas City.

Subsequent to this position, I worked for a privately owned franchise in the mall owned by a husband and wife team. They were a train wreck. I was given the position of vice president of development, but I soon realized they didn't need me yet and were not big enough to keep me busy. To justify my pay, I did everything from running for supplies to writing manuals, leasing space, and working in their stores. But I was constantly caught between the two of them.

After a year, I knew it was time to move on. A friend of mine called to say there was a job opening for an assistant manager at a mall in Littleton. She thought I would be a good match. The general manager, Pat, phoned and invited me for an interview. I knew when I talked with him, it was a good fit. His job had lost excitement, and he wanted to train me to take over so he could move on to his next role, whatever that was going to be. He was tired of working and trained me for his position as general manager. Pat trained me well by basically letting me run everything. I had a great experience and worked with some wonderful, fun people.

After two years of no openings for mall management positions in Denver shopping malls for me to move into, Pat called me into his office and gave me a reference for a job that was perfect for me. The job was local, and the company was out of Memphis. They wanted to start an open-air mall. It was a new concept at that time, and there were restaurants and upscale stores. When I met with the regional manager, I thought it sounded perfect. We got off to a good start in July of 2001. However, in the midst of starting at this new position, the tragedy of September 11th happened, and that caused a struggle for our shopping center.

Because the concept of the open-air mall was still so new, I was able to give jobs to some of my own professionally qualified contacts. I enjoyed my time there. I was soon managing three shopping centers and even went to Memphis to run their flagship mall. I loved going to Memphis to visit but didn't want to move there.

Since the mall was privately owned, we struggled to get financing. The owners ended up partnering with another company that had the option to purchase the mall after a set number of years. My positive experience with the company was crushed when they were bought out, and I didn't want to be involved with the purchasing company.

In 2003, I transferred to one of the three shopping centers I was running in Colorado Springs, which was wholly owned by the family-owned company I had started with. I continued commuting there from my home in south Denver until 2004 when they hired a man named Dean, whom I later called a "pathetic excuse for a human being." He earned this name after I had several run-ins with him, during which he would yell, scream and use obscenities until I relented and gave him his way. The worst of this was once when I was in a car with him driving. He became enraged because a security person motioned for him to slow down in a construction zone. He floored the gas pedal, screeched the tires and almost hit the man. I was terrified! It was nothing but his way, with no discussion. It was awful, but it was the impetus for me to decide to go to school for my residential real estate license and transition out of my 15-year commercial real estate career.

While I was in real estate classes a few years later, I wasn't sure what to do professionally. Then, a couple of doors opened for me to work in residential real estate. I was still working in commercial real estate but I was no longer happy there. I was aware that my hard work was lining corporate pockets. Dean was looking through our commercial leases to find every way he could to twist the language and cheat our tenants out of more money to add to the bottom line and make himself look good. I was being asked daily to lie, cheat, and steal, and I couldn't do it. I also began to realize I wanted to help people on a more individual basis. I couldn't figure out why, exactly, but it felt like serving people individually would have more meaning and be more fulfilling.

At the same time, I began work on my first investment property and finished the process of getting my residential real estate license. One of my instructors at real estate school had an entry-level opening in a title company within a locally owned mortgage company. The company consisted of a father and his sons, who were also my neighbors. During my interview, they asked me what my goals were. I didn't even hesitate to say that I wanted to build my own real estate company. I had never been so bold before. They responded with, "Well, good for you," and said I could work on my real estate career while I worked for them—making sure the work for them was done first. I wasn't big on the idea of owning my own company for my real estate business at first, but my boyfriend convinced me it was a good idea. I took the position, knowing I could do my best serving people if I learned everything about the business from the ground up.

In 2005, I received my real estate license from the State of Colorado, and I worked at the title company while I built my real estate business over the following 12 months. Doing this sharpened my time management and organizational skills. I then worked with two real estate brokerage firms over the next two years: the first one, a small "boutique" firm, and then a company called Metro Brokers where I worked on a team owned by one of my real estate school instructors. My good friend Jennifer then introduced me to Keller Williams (KW). It took me a while, but I realized that KW was the right company for me to partner with.

Something about working in real estate changed me. It went beyond learning to run my own business and becoming an entrepreneur. I figured out how to serve people well. I understood why I wanted to serve them: I wanted to make a difference in the lives of others. In fact, today I grow frustrated when I can't help people. Keller Williams supported my service through their philosophy and values, and I always have felt supported as an individual there.

KW cofounder Gary Keller, in his book The Millionaire Real Estate Agent, refers to the "big why," or the reason you get out of bed each day. It wasn't about the money for me; it was about serving people. The "big why" helped me realize that I wanted to make a difference for people. Up to that point my career motives had been more on the spectrum of being self-absorbed. When I embraced faith and service to others, it brought me past the fear and uncertainty of having my own business and not having the guarantee of a regular paycheck, insurance, or retirement. I needed to place my trust outside of myself and outside of my smaller worldly sphere. I needed, once again, to let go of the illusion of control and to remember there is a plan greater than any I could try to control—trust in God. At that point in my life, I didn't want to work for someone who was not in line with my spiritual beliefs. In Keller Williams, I found the same values and philosophies I cherished.

I did not grow up being exposed to spirituality. Religion had been shoved down my mom's throat when she was young and she didn't want to do the same to us. We never went to church. Mom figured we could ask questions and discover our own path, and it would be up to us to decide. I would sometimes go to church services with my friends and talk with them about what they believed in. Still, I never really understood what they were talking about.

It was my friend, Jenn, who had helped me find my faith in 2006. She had been raised by a Baptist preacher. She would ask me difficult questions about faith and God as we skied together. Eventually, this simple experience of asking questions as we spent time together brought an epiphany into the essential meaning of faith for me. Over the next year, I started attending Bible study and asked even more questions. I started trusting in faith, and it became an integral part of my being.

While pondering this new awareness of faith and spirituality, I often wondered what it would be like to experience the Ironman myself, but I never put much faith in my ability to reach this level. I considered myself merely a recreational athlete, not at the level of a professional athlete. I was never a swimmer and I didn't start mountain biking until I was 30 years old. The only part of Ironman I thought I could do was run, and though I ran the Pikes Peak ascent, I had never run anything longer. The Ironman became a castle in the clouds, and though I had fleeting thoughts about racing, I always talked myself out of pursuing it.

Growing Faith

In February 2012, I was struggling in my personal life. My husband and I were in the midst of a contentious divorce, each represented by attorneys and attempting to settle using a mediator. Even though I summoned the immense energy it took to continually deal with this toxicity, I began to feel empty and alone, like a child without a father. It was a strange and yet familiar feeling; strange because it was a new experience of being alone, without a partner. Familiar, because I had known it in childhood when I was without my biological dad.

The first time I heard the term "Father" in reference to God was from a dear friend of mine, Sandy, who was the team leader at a neighboring Keller Williams office. We were at a Keller Williams conference, and I awoke crying. I put on my game face to be with the lead agents and guests I had invited. We all sat together, but Sandy could see that I was hurting. She took me aside and asked me what was going on. I asked who was going to ever love me after my divorce, and she offered to pray with me.

I started crying, so she grabbed my hand and we went to the ladies room together. I was nervous and scared. I felt broken and recognized I had nothing to lose by going with her. We ended up going into the handicapped stall. I started sobbing so strongly that my entire body shook. She put her hands on my shoulders and whispered a beautiful prayer in my ear. She asked our Father to put His arms around me, be my companion, and lead me through this time in life. She asked Him to show me beauty and strength and to lead me down the path He created for me that would lead to His kingdom.

I immediately felt a sense of peace overcome me and slowly stopped sobbing. We prayed together, and I walked out feeling a sense of peace and newfound strength. I'll always be grateful she helped open my mind and spirit to a new relationship with God. What I came to understand from that sense of peace and strength was that praying doesn't change things; rather, prayer changes us, and then we make changes.

Through the whole process of focusing on my dream and going through what I needed to go through to train to get there, my faith grew. I realized what faith did for me.

In the beginning, I had to have faith that I would get there, and I asked God for help. Twice a day, I prayed for the resources, strength and perseverance to achieve my dream. Then, when it got hard, I would ask God for help. I would ask Him, "What do I do here? I am really struggling." Then I would hear or feel His answer somewhere in my day, and overwhelming comfort and peace would ensue. This is how my faith grew into a relationship with God. I never would have seen it in this light had it not been for this dream and for the deep pain and struggle I went through. I am forever grateful and give thanks often for this gift.

VERBALIZATION / MAKE A DECISION

Chapter 6

The Decision

A t the beginning of September 2010, I was seriously thinking about going to Kona. When I talked with my husband about it, he thought I was crazy. His view was that a person didn't just roll out of bed one day and decide to go to Kona. He had two friends who had been trying to get to Kona for ten years. I took in all he said, and I could still picture myself in Kona. I could see myself there and imagine what it would smell like and feel like. Ultimately, I told myself, Okay, I'm going to pursue this.

My preparation for Kona changed everything in my life. My personal relationships changed and my marriage changed. Allen had been an adventure racer and was, frankly, done with that part of his life. He knew the hours, days, and commitment that came with it, and he didn't want any part of it. He seemed to want a more traditional wife, and he flat out told me I couldn't do it.

I was inconsolable with his discouragement. I began to want Kona more than anything, maybe even more than my marriage. I didn't know what to do. I felt terrible; I told my husband he was crushing that dream. Perhaps I had not been able to verbalize it before or truly realize it, but Kona was now my dream. It was my lifelong dream, and my husband didn't understand my devastation.

That night, I asked God what to do since my pursuit of Kona might put a strain on my marriage. As I prayed, words came to me ever so gently. They said that I needed to live my dreams and walk my path.

Part of the subsequent process of preparing for Kona included talking to God on a more regular basis, which helped my emotional and mental stamina. Prayer helped me through difficult times in my marriage and long days of training. I prayed every morning and night for the strength to do what was needed to rise up and walk on the path that God intended. I thanked God for the blessings He brought to my life, for the people He placed on my journey, and for showing me the way.

The next day, I told my husband I knew he didn't understand, but I needed to pursue Kona. Even if I couldn't succeed, I needed to try. I trusted myself. My husband asked his friends who were pursuing Kona over to talk some sense into me. They supported my husband's viewpoint. Although they admitted I was in good shape, they asked what made me think I could get there. Part of it was they wondered what gave me the audacity to think I could make it to Kona when they had been trying for ten years. They just didn't believe in me.

After making the decision to train for the Ironman triathlon in Kona, Hawaii, I shared the news with my friends and family. Verbalizing my plan made me more accountable not just to others, but to myself and God. My two main supporters in my pursuit of the Ironman were my sister, Ruby, and my best friend, Crystal. They did not even blink an eye when I told them I wanted to participate in the Ironman. Ruby said she knew without a doubt that I would get there. Ruby and

Crystal both jumped in to help me achieve my dream. They were there if I needed them and lifted me up whenever I was down. Ruby and Crystal bought me gear from Ironman events and would wake before dawn to help me at triathlons.

Crystal became my best friend, and it's funny for me to look back at the first time we met. I'm reminded how inaccurate first impressions can be. It was our mutual friend, Jenn, the one who had brought me to Keller Williams, who introduced us and invited us both to her in-laws' cabin outside of Crested Butte. There were a dozen or so people coming as friends of the family. Jenn and Crystal were busily chatting, which they love to do. I happened to overhear their political conversation. I absolutely HATE discussing politics. Crystal struck me as somewhat of a conspiracy theorist about our country and government, and I didn't like that, either. She ended up having to leave the weekend early, and I was glad she did. Later, I realized that the problem was my own fear that Crystal was smarter than me, knowing all about politics and conspiracy theories as she did, that made me not like her. I always wondered whether people that knew stuff like that knew something I didn't and would be the ones to be able to get away to safety in the face of some U.S. catastrophe I wasn't even aware of.

Shortly after that weekend, I invited Jenn to go skiing several times, but she was never available. She told me Crystal was available and wanted to go skiing, as well. She suggested we go together, and added that she thought Crystal and I were a lot alike—Crystal was warm, smart, and funny, with a big heart and a fantastic sense of humor. She said she thought we would hit it off and become friends. Wanting to get better at skiing and knowing the key to it was going more often, I called Crystal. She was agreeable and wanted to get better at skiing, too. Turns out, we were both licensed real estate agents, working with different companies. She had worked on investment properties and so had I. Additionally, we were both striving to improve in skiing and were about the same level.

On our way up the hill, we realized we had more in common. We had both started our careers in retail—I worked in stores and she was a buyer. I had always wanted to be a buyer! We also discussed our spirituality and our growing faith. I found out she wasn't as politically radical as I thought; it was my own insecurity of not knowing much of anything in that world that had me thinking she was more politically inclined.

I was astounded at how well read Crystal was, and I loved both her intellect and her drive to learn and do more. She also made me laugh! To this day, she cracks me up all the time. Her humor is smart and intelligent. She travels a lot. That she has been so willing to accommodate her own travel schedule to come support me in my training speaks to her dedication as a true friend.

It's been rare for me to meet people who are absolutely true to their word and this is both my sister Ruby and my friend Crystal. We can say anything to each other and it is safe. We strive to realize our potential and will point out things to one another that no one else will. We each bring something to the other. Their support of me has been huge in my being able to put my pursuit of my dream of being an athlete who could compete in the Kona Ironman World Championship.

I had been an athlete my entire life and had done some races in the past, but I didn't have an athletic "resume." I had done the Pikes Peak Ascent half-marathon. I had also done the Bolder Boulder five times.

The Bolder Boulder is one of my favorite races of all time. It is a 10k race through the streets of Boulder, Colorado, ending in the University of Colorado Stadium to cheering crowds. Boulder has a very bohemian feel, and this translates to the race, which is why it has always been one of my favorites. It draws some 50,000 runners and international pros that win money for top place finishes. Along the route, there is entertainment that has grown organically over the years. Many people wear costumes and provide the runners a little coolness with sprinklers and sprayers as they go by. Fraternity and sorority members turn out on the lawns of their houses, cheering for runners. Bands play music on stage during the race. There are cheerleaders and high-school bands. It's a real festival. Your mind is concentrating on the spectacle you are seeing so you don't think about the running very much. Plus, with 50,000 runners, you can't even hear yourself breathe. It is spectacularly fun!

I'd also done several races of 10k or less and two sprint triathlons in years prior: Tri for the Cure twice, with distances of 0.47 miles, swim; 12 miles, bike; and 3.2 miles, run. I had experience in mountain biking, and I thought that road biking was boring, so I had no experience with it.

Chapter 7

Can I Compete?

A t the beginning of my intense training for the Kona IM WC and after a coach had agreed to take me on, I underwent medical testing to make sure I was physically capable of completing the training and the race. I had made the decision to go for it, and I had committed to train. Now I had to make sure my body was capable of doing the necessary work.

Crystal came along to see what this VO2 Max thing was all about (VO2 Max refers to the maximum amount of oxygen that an individual can utilize during maximum or intense exercise.) Her presence there was reassuring for me. I knew she could pick up anything I didn't hear in my excitement to be officially pursuing my dream.

The doctor was a pro cycling team physician. He had been the team race doctor for the Garmin team and thus had prominent athletes as patients. In his office, he had many signed and framed Tour de France team jerseys, which I thought was great! His office was in central Denver, and his testing laboratory was a big room with several stationary bikes, treadmills, padded exam tables, black fabric covered partitions to section off each testing area, a clean white tile floor and lots of ground-level windows with metal blinds, most of them shut. He ran two tests: the VO2 max and lactic acid threshold tests. The VO2 max determined my maximum oxygen absorption; if it was too low, I wouldn't be able to compete in Ironman races because of the physical strain. The lactic acid processing test showed how efficient my muscles were at processing lactic acid, which builds up in the muscles and often causes cramping that can stop or slow endurance athletes down. I once watched a movie called "American Flyers" that depicted this scenario.

During my testing, I completed increasingly difficult intervals on the bike and then ran on the treadmill. Every few minutes, the doctor would draw blood by pricking my ear or finger to evaluate the oxygen and lactic acid levels in my bloodstream. I had to do both tests wearing a plastic mask that measured my oxygen intake and the output of carbon monoxide. It was hard to exercise with the plastic mask covering most of my face. Ironically, it made me feel like I couldn't breathe. The doctor also did a caliper test to determine my body fat percentage and my heart rate training zones. The lower zones were for burning fat and building endurance, while those in higher ranges helped build lung capacity and speed.

After the doctor finished the testing, he took Crystal and me into his office to show us the results. He said my score was high enough to complete the Ironman, but just barely over the mark needed. Since I had been an athlete my entire life, he expected my scores to be higher. He compared my results to some of the top endurance athletes and explained how they could keep going for longer periods of time. Their bodies could process high levels of oxygen and were efficient in taking glucose from food to turn it into fuel to repair muscle, gain energy, and wash away lactic acid efficiently. He said he could tell with near perfect certainty who could win an endurance event after testing their lactic acid efficiency since those athletes were able to continue without severe muscle fatigue.

My results paled in comparison to the top athletes—but this didn't deter me. I was energized and couldn't wait to start training. My coach asked for my VO2 max score and heart rate training zones so she could know where to start training. The tests would determine how much progress I needed to make and what kind of training schedule I needed in order to prepare for the Kona races and the Ironman training season. It was important for me to do some low level base training, which consists of long and slow fat-burning training sessions. These help build new mitochondria in the lungs so when you layer on a higher mileage and pace, the body can deal with it. I would need to ramp up my training during the months of January through May.

Because of the testing, the doctor gave me something called heart rate zones for which I needed a watch and heart rate monitor strap. Heart rate training zones are calculated by taking into consideration your Maximum Heart Rate (HRmax) and your Resting Heart Rate (HRrest). Within each training zone, subtle physiological effects take place to enhance your fitness.

Once I had the tests done, I decided to buy an expensive Garmin watch to monitor heart-training zones and send the data from workouts back to my coach. It would also track the distance, pace, and calories burned for each discipline. The only problem was that it was big, bulky, and heavy, and felt like a brick on my arm.

Making the decision to follow my dream was the first step. Through these medical tests, I had taken the next step in the decision—finding out if I had the capacity! And knowing I had the capacity, I set out on one of the hardest parts of my journey—conquering my beliefs about myself that limited me and held me back.

CONQUER LIMITING BELIEFS

Chapter 8

My First Official Ironman Event, Lubbock, TX

In June 2011, I participated in an official Ironman event to try and grab a qualifying spot to be able to compete in Kona. These spots were only offered at a handful of races, and this one was a half-Ironman distance called Buffalo Springs because of the town within Lubbock, Texas where the race is held. It sounded like a good race to compete in since I could drive to it with my bike, instead of having to pay to transport it or break it down and ship it.

I had a personal goal, too. Because this was the race where a teammate, a woman being coached alongside me by my coach—someone I'd come to regard as my "nemesis" and given the made-up name "Peyton"—took the spot the year before. I met her with the hope I could learn from her but ended up strongly disliking her for her attitudes toward the sports that I held so dear. I used my dislike for her as a driving force and said, "If she can do this Ironman, so can I."

I knew I needed to start somewhere; therefore, I didn't do much research on the race. My coach had told me it would be hot and somewhat hilly, and I thought it would be my kind of race! I love the challenge of hills and racing in heat—even extreme heat. I have always excelled in hot conditions rather than cold.

My coach had been incorporating hills in my running and biking training to get me to be faster at them. She said running and biking were where I could blow by other athletes. Sounded good to me! I felt healthy, lean, and grateful that I had no training or completion injuries. Still, I was a bit scared thinking of all the contingencies to overcome, like those in the Moab race. So I followed everything my coach said, to the letter. She set up a pre-race lunch with me a week or so before my departure and took me step by step through everything I needed, including nutrition, supplements, contingencies, recovery supplies, and clothing. Then we went through the pre- and post-race activities at an Ironman.

I was ecstatic to be going to my first official Ironman race! I would be with like-minded athletes and could buy official merchandise to my heart's content! There are only a handful of sanctioned Ironman races where athletes can qualify for the Ironman World Championship in Kona. Since the 1990s, non-sanctioned races have popped up—with different cutoff times than sanctioned events. In response, the World Triathlon Corporation registered the trademark for the "Ironman Triathlon" and the "Ironman" and owns rights to putting those names on clothing, athletic equipment, souvenirs, and other items.

When the week came for me to travel to Texas for the race, I had so much to do between work and race preparation. I felt mentally exhausted and overwhelmed trying to remember details. I felt like I had reached my limit because everything peaked at once: training, work, sleep deprivation, pushing my body to the limit, preparing everything for the race, checking and re-checking weather forecasts, thinking through the race over and over, visualizing how I wanted the day to go, and reviewing all the "what-if" scenarios. I started feeling like I was losing my mind.

Lubbock was plain, small, hot, and desolate; not something pretty to look at, like Colorado. Nevertheless, I was excited to be there because this could be where my vision became reality! I felt like I was finally on the road to my dreams, and I would get to test everything I had been doing in training. I would also get to see professional Ironman athletes and observe how they raced. I could barely contain my excitement!

I wanted to go right to the lake and racecourse, so Allan and I did, stopping first at a little convenience store. I had been carefully watching everything I ate and drank leading up to the race: no dairy or alcohol, very little fat. Basically, I was eating salads with lots of veggies, fruits, and carbs. I went in and grabbed a big bottle of water and some pretzels. When I got in line to pay, two slender people in their seventies with athletic race shirts were in line, too. I could tell they were triathletes and struck up a conversation. They said they had participated in the race before and asked whether I had. They said it was a nice race and a good place to grab Kona spots. That immediately struck a chord with me. I told them that I had come to do just that, and then we wished each other good luck. I felt like I was where I needed to be to reach my goals.

Then I saw what they were buying—soda and moon pies! I was flabbergasted! I had been very meticulous about my nutrition since deciding to train and compete for Kona. There they were, 25 years older and getting ready to eat processed junk food. I stood there in complete shock and thought Well, I'll show them! I will be faster and healthier.

Back in the car, my husband and I decided to take a drive to the lake and transition area. Next, I wanted to drive the course. This is standard practice for triathletes to work out your strategy of when to accelerate and when to conserve energy. The lake was pretty, and the houses around it were nice but not overly opulent. The water was decently clear and sparkled in the sunlight. The transition area was being set up beside the lake. I spotted the giant hill to climb—right out of transition—to access the bike course that my coach and other athletes and had been right to warn me about. It was big, but I wasn't worried. I thought,

Ah, I will still be fresh, so I will be fine. There were a few trees in the lake area, but none to speak of on the course. The weather forecast for race day called for 100-plus degrees. I wasn't daunted; I was thrilled at the thought of having a challenging race for my first Ironman. Bring it on, I thought.

The bike course was a maze of twists and turns on two-lane rural roads with little shoulder, and it was constantly windy. This wasn't cool wind as in Colorado, either. It was hot wind and felt like the rush of blazing air when you open the oven door. We had to do only one loop on the course, and I was happy about that. If it was windy on race day, I would probably only have to endure wind at certain points on the loop and not have to be in it constantly.

We drove the run course, which exited the lake in the opposite direction of the bike course and was an out-and-back with some hills. It had a turnaround by a power plant on a flat stretch of completely desolate road. I realized it would be the hottest part of the day by the time I was on the run course. Staying on top of hydration and not allowing my temperature to rise too high would be key. I wanted to get in the lake and do a short swim workout and then go back to the hotel and check in. We parked by what would be the finish line, where the other triathletes were, and I started changing behind the car door into my bikini to go under my wet suit. I had no problem taking off and putting on clothes behind only my car door. My husband came over and asked, alarmed, what I was doing. I explained that everyone else was doing the same thing and they weren't watching me. If they were, they would get a quick show but everyone has the same anatomy, and mine was no different than anyone else's. I could tell he disapproved.

I put on my wet suit and asked for his help zipping up the back. As he zipped it, he noticed two big holes on each side of the zipper at the base. I told him to stop messing around because that would freak me out. My wet suit was brand new. I could tell by his facial expression that he was serious, so I asked him to describe the size and shape of the holes and whether they were all the way through the suit. Both were pretty deep, he said, but not all the way through the last layer of neoprene and mesh (Thank God!), and were the size of a quarter. I was dumbstruck and wondered how in the heck they had gotten there. I even wondered if my husband had made them on purpose to get me not to race!

I brought myself back to focus on the workout at hand, after which I could deal with repairing the holes. I grabbed the rest of my gear and made my way down to the lake. The water was clear and refreshing and other triathletes were getting in. Many weren't even bothering with a wet suit, and all of them were talking about whether we'd be allowed to wear them since it had been so hot there. The rule about wearing wet suits in a race is this: the director reads the water temperature in the middle of the lake at 3 a.m. on the day of the race, and if it is warmer than 76.1 degrees F, wet suits are not allowed. Athletes who still want to wear them are allowed to race but are not eligible for awards because of the unfair advantage the additional flotation gives them over the rest of the field.

I hadn't thought very much about the possibility of not being able to wear my wet suit, and I grew fearful about that happening. I was already a tentative swimmer and felt better swimming with my wet suit. It made it easier to stay afloat, which always felt like my biggest problem in having a smooth stroke.

As I did my practice swim, I concentrated on every part of my stroke and tried to feel at one with the water. To quiet my mind over the wet suit worry, I told myself I could call my coach for advice when I got to the hotel. After doing so, I realized that worry was simply a limiting belief, and I could re-wire it by concentrating on the task at hand, being fully present, and telling myself it would all work out for race day. It worked. My swim went well and the water felt so good that I forgot about the holes in my wet suit. I stopped to look at where the race buoys would probably be set in a triangular pattern and practiced making left-hand turns to simulate turning at the buoys. I exited the water feeling good and was ready to get to the hotel, unpack my stuff, get something to eat, and call my coach.

I took off my wet suit to get a look at the holes and saw that my zipper likely caused them when I folded the wet suit to pack it. Dang it! Already a big snag. I wondered if the holes would get worse, letting water into my wet suit and causing me to sink. I didn't wait until we got to the hotel to call my coach, Gretchen.

She got on the phone and calmed me down, explaining there should be rubber cement products at the Ironman Expo taking place in the hotel that could fix my suit. I asked her if it would work with the race so close, and she assured me it would. Whew! She also reiterated what I had already thought about the run portion of the race and weather forecast. She emphasized the importance of getting water at every station and putting it on my head early—it could make the difference between finishing and not.

She then asked how prepared I was for the race, logistically. Particularly, she asked about my liquid nutrition, Infinit, and what I was going to eat for breakfast before the race. Infinit is really cool stuff; it's a powder that you mix with water that you can customize for how much carbohydrate and protein you want for the distance of your race. This was my first race using it, so to not leave anything to chance, I had pre-mixed two full bottles of it (one as a back-up) and left the big bag of powder at home. This was bad news, my coach said. The protein becomes active once the powder is mixed with the water and might mold in the two nights and one day before the race. Oh no! When I told her I hadn't brought the bag with me, she told me I now had another thing to find in the Expo or in the town of Lubbock. She tried to calm my nerves by explaining that with so many triathletes in town, there was bound to be a store or vendor with some Infinit I could buy. I tried to believe it would be okay, but I was secretly breaking into a sweat. This was a tough limiting belief to change because I had put so much importance on supplements. What I didn't realize yet was it was my mindset that drove physical ability, not supplements.

After I got off the phone, I informed my husband of our new priority of finding Infinit and wet suit cement. I then high-tailed it down to the Expo. I found the wet suit cement right off—that was easy. The sellers explained how to use the applicator brush and to pinch the opening together so each side of the fabric was flush and liberally apply the cement. I would have to apply four coats so it would be waterproof, and I needed drying time in between coats. That meant I had to hurry and apply the first two coats before bed and the remaining coats the next day in order to be ready for the race.

Finding the Infinit was another matter. I checked every vendor and not only did no one have it, they hadn't even heard of it. I couldn't see how that was possible. Vendors tried to sell me on their product, but my coach's words rang in my ears: "Never try anything new on race day. You're just asking for trouble since your system isn't used to it." I began to panic. My eye wandered for a second to some really cool Ironman race t-shirts that were my red and black race colors with a fantastic logo of Buffalo Springs. While buying one, I found that the girls selling them were local. I asked them about local triathlon stores and they gave me two names. I ran upstairs as quickly as I could to look up the numbers in the telephone book. Although I caught them just before closing, they too had not heard of Infinit. Now I really began to sweat!

I ran back downstairs to check the vendors one more time. I found the Mark Allen booth, and that seemed hopeful since he was one of the inventors of Infinit. The young woman was closing up, but I caught her attention and told her what I needed. She said they had protein powder, but not the Infinit product line. I asked if she knew if another product at the expo might be close in content. She didn't know.

With no choices left, I went back upstairs to my room feeling like I had completely messed up and might have ruined my chances to qualify for Kona in my first official race. I called my coach again, and she couldn't believe no one had it. I asked her if she was sure that the protein would go bad by race day and she said it would be worse to chance it than try something else. She suggested PowerBar, Hammer, or Gatorade, Gatorade being last on the list due to the sugar content. I had tried Hammer before and although I wanted to use it and liked the products, they did not agree with my stomach. I loved the PowerBar gels, so thought this might be a good choice. Since the expo was now closed for the evening, I would buy it in the morning.

That night, there was a mandatory pre-race meeting. Before every race, the head referee goes over the rules. Then the race director delivers his message to the athletes. He started talking and welcomed everyone to the 18th year of the race. He looked like Kris Kristofferson and spoke slowly with a pronounced Texas drawl. The athlete I sat next to at the meeting had competed in many Ironman events and groused about having to attend all of the pre-race meetings because they repeated a lot of the same information: "We will let you know on race day about wet suits; don't draft on the bike; no electronic devices of any kind and no crossing the finish line with your family." It was all new to me, and I hung on every word.

The meeting went exactly as the athlete said and had more detail and redundancy than I thought humanly possible. The cycling referee made his point several times about getting either time penalties or total disqualification for drafting. Drafting is what they do in the peloton in the Tour de France. It's why they all ride so tightly; they can use less energy by having another person break the wind first, making it easier on the riders behind. Since Ironman sees this as an unfair advantage, there are no-drafting rules, complete with how far riders have to space themselves and how to overtake (pass) another rider. And my personal favorite: If a female rider wants to pass a male rider, he has to let her pass and cannot block her or speed up to prevent her from doing so. I could see how this could happen with egomaniacal male athletes who don't like getting "chicked" by a faster female athlete. But this was the Ironman, and all involved wanted to make it a level playing field. The scarier thing for me was that I could be penalized for unknowingly being in front of a rider who was within drafting zone of my back wheel. I didn't like that rule at all! I had enough going on, looking ahead, without being concerned about who was behind me and how close they were.

After the athlete meeting had stretched on for over two hours, people began to leave. I wanted to make sure I didn't miss anything, but since the athlete next to me departed, so did I. It was past 8:30 p.m., and every long-distance triathlete knows that 8:30 at night is when we hit the wall and have to go to bed. Besides, I still needed to put another coat of rubber cement on my wet suit.

The day before the race meant race packet pick-up and the athlete dinner. I needed to do a couple of pre-race workouts to keep my muscles ready and test the repair job I'd done on the wet suit. I couldn't pick up my packet until 1 p.m., so I headed out to get breakfast and then to the lake to do my workouts. At the hotel restaurant, we had one of the greasiest breakfasts known to humankind. I don't know how scrambled eggs and dry toast can be made greasy, but they were and it didn't agree with my stomach. Lesson learned: It is imperative when you are relying on your body to perform at a high level on demand that you be sure about the food at the restaurants near the race location. If you're not, bring your own food!

We went to the lake, and I tested the wet suit. It was as solid as could be. Whew! Now I had to hope the temperature cooperated enough for me to wear it. I did a quick 15-minute swim to warm up my muscles and limber up my joints and then went to the car to change into biking clothes before doing a short ride. Pre-race day, you always do workouts in the same order as the race and visualize all parts of the race, the entries and the exits in efficient transitions, and a solid finish. When out on my bike, I saw every kind of tri bike imaginable. The air was energized. The pros were warming up and my excitement grew. As I finished, the wind came up, which I figured would also happen on race day. I visualized welcoming a cooling wind—I was really trying to play a trick on my mind.

When I looked at my watch, I realized I was going to head out for my run at roughly the same time during the race the next day. I thought my trial run would be a good gauge for how hot it would feel. I made friends with the wind, remembered all the things the referee said about the rules, then stopped at the car and changed into my running gear. I wanted to do my run on part of a big hill that was just outside the lake entrance and would be at the beginning and end of the run segment.

I finished my run with the wind blowing like a heater. I thought it was a good thing I liked the heat! With that, I packed up my stuff and headed back to the hotel, showered and made my way to the huge line that went out the front door of the hotel to pick up my athlete packet. After an hour in line, I made it to the assembly-line process. First, they check your name and U.S. Triathlon Association membership. They find your packet by identifying your name with a race number. In the packet are your race bib and equipment, transition stickers, swim cap (a different color is used for each wave to track people and age group/gender), timing chip strap, and official athlete wristband. In this case, the packet had temporary race number tattoos. Some races do this and others mark directly on the athletes on race day with permanent marker. Once you get your race packet, you get a timing chip. It is tested to make sure it is active and corresponds with your name and race number. Then you start the process of putting your race number on everything: bike helmet, bike, transition area, race shirt or race belt, swim cap, etc., so your number is on you at all times during the race.

After this, you go through the painstaking process of going through all your gear, item by item, to make sure everything is in good working order, free of holes or loose parts, and that you have a backup for everything—just in case.

I never enjoyed this process because I worried there was something I was not thinking of and all would go wrong on race day. Then, for added fun, I actually went through everything that might possibly go wrong and scenarios of how to handle it. It was a new way to conquer the limiting belief of what have I forgotten: I simply faced it! I figured that if doing my same pre-race routine wasn't serving the outcome I wanted, I could change it. So I did, and it felt so much better. By this time, I was both keyed up about racing and anxious to get it over with. I could hardly sit still. By then, it was time for the athlete pre-race dinner.

The entire main floor of the hotel was filled with round tables for the triathletes. I was amazed at the large number of participants in the race and then realized many had guests or family with them, as well. It was still an impressively sized group. There was a buffet of carb-laden food—and tons of it! Since there is some evidence that pre-race carb-loading helps performance, many endurance athletes endorse the practice. The Ironman pre-race dinner was no exception. I had plenty of pasta, bread, rice and anything else I could stuff in my face, not really knowing how much energy I would need for the next day. I found a place to sit next to the experienced Ironman from the pre-athlete meeting. We talked about Ironman races that he and his brother had done.

There was a full presentation while we were finishing our meal. One thing it highlighted was the youngest and oldest athletes in the race. The youngest was Drew Scott, son of one of my icons from having watched the Ironman coverage for 20-plus years—Dave Scott. Dave came up to the podium to talk briefly about his experiences in Ironman. He said how proud he was to have his son participate, having coached him. I was enthralled! There he was: casual, unassuming, and open. He joked around, poking fun at his son, saying he hoped everything he had told him in coaching had gotten through. Wow! The magical feeling of the Ironman swept over me and I knew everything was going to be okay.

How the roll-down process would work for Kona and the Half Ironman championships in Las Vegas were explained in the presentation. A qualifying spot could roll down to the next athlete behind a fast one who had earned but declined it. A limited number of championship spots existed for both the full and half Ironman finals. Top finishers who had qualified for the spots would be called to the stage to decide whether or not to take their spot. Personally, I couldn't fathom how there could be any question! If they did not take a spot, it would "roll down" to the next qualifying athlete. My coach had told me to make sure I was there for this. It would be the way I would get my spot if I didn't finish in the top of my age group. I was skeptical about anyone not taking a spot and giving me a roll-down opportunity, but my newfound Ironman friend assured me that it happened frequently because there were other races athletes had already committed to. Not all athletes care about going to the championships, especially if they have been before. Also, there was a hefty $750 entry fee for Kona, and $500 for Las Vegas, plus travel, accommodations, bike shipping, and time off of work. You had to pay immediately to take the spot; if you didn't, the spot rolled down to the next person who would.

Feeling confident in my understanding of the process, I excused myself to go up to the room, do final race prep for the next day, and attempt to force myself to sleep. Sleep just doesn't happen the night before a race. Between excitement, anticipation, and endless "what if" scenarios, it is hard to sleep. You end up sleeping for small stretches of time, only to wake up with a different thought about the race. Finally, when you are worn out enough to get into some real sleep, it's 3:45 a.m. and time to get up. As a triathlete, you have to get used to getting up in the dark and getting your body and mind ready to perform. Race day is the culmination of this type of training over time.

Before bed, I would go through every inch of a race in my mind while looking at each corresponding piece of equipment to make sure everything was ready. I tired quickly of this process, while for others it seemed to be their strong suit. Since I'm a positive thinker, I'm bad at thinking of all of the bad things that could happen and the contingencies I'd need to get through them. This contingency process has, therefore, been an important part of the experience and training I gained through racing.

I was awake before the alarm went off. I got up to start putting water and fuel in my system far enough ahead of the race start to have it fully digested by then. If I didn't, I would have digestion and performance problems during the race. You don't want to eat too much or too little; it's a fine line of what, when, and how much you eat. For my pre-race meal, I ate two hard-boiled eggs, water, two pieces of cinnamon swirl toast, my typical vitamin supplements, and some Lance Armstrong EFS energy drink. The thoughts of the "what-if" scenarios that had been popping into my head all night continued after I got up to start preparing for the race. I had this constant state of feeling scared and excited—90 percent scared, 10 percent excited! This was also how I used to feel when I first started mountain biking on single-track. It scared me more than excited me, but I knew if I pushed through it, I would eventually turn it around to 90 percent excited, 10 percent scared. I went through my pre-race morning routine: take a quick shower, put on my race kit (outfit), stretch out my entire body, use a foam roller to roll out any stiff or sore spots—all the while feeling like the new person at work who doesn't quite know what's going on and puts up a good front. To change this dreaded feeling, I verbalized opposite thoughts: I am a good runner, I am a strong swimmer, I have completed all of the training that will bring success…and these new thoughts slowly evaporated the scared feeling, transforming it into confidence!

Usually, you either leave your stuff secured in the transition area overnight or you take it and sort out your transition area as soon as it opens, between 5 and 6 a.m. You also want to do short warm-ups for all three events—swim, bike, and run—but the swim part has to be last, because you go right to the start line. This means timing out everything really well, including how many times you will need to go to the bathroom before putting on your wet suit for the swim warm-up and start, and approximating how long the lines for port-o-lets will be. You always add in some extra time, just in case. This also means you have down time if everything goes faster than planned, which is not great because your mind starts going into overdrive.

Finally, it was time to pack up all my gear and drive to the race area. It was still completely dark outside when we left the hotel. I could tell it was going to be a scorcher, which excited me. There was a slight smell of cow pastures, and all was quiet except for the sound of triathletes quietly carrying gear to their cars. Driving to the race area was surreal. The exit ramp was completely backed up; it seemed like a weekend night after a concert, rather than 4:30 a.m. before the sun was up. The race volunteers had the athletes park far away from the start and transition, which meant having to carry all my stuff in the dark. I was thinking, Will I be running or biking or swimming right next to this person that I'm walking beside now? Are they faster than me or am I faster than them? Then I would size them up by their physique. Were they skinny, did they have some extra pounds? I was trying to see a physical weakness that I could exploit if I came across them during the race. All of this was just mental mind games because there was no way I'd ever remember or recognize any of these people later in the race. Trying to size people up by their physicality is impossible. Plenty of times at the pool, I'd see overweight swimmers who could swim for hours and leave me behind in a flash!

Next, I found out that the trek would be down that big, challenging hill we saw the first day, and I worried about tripping or injuring myself or my stuff. Luckily, other athletes had thought to bring headlamps, which I mentally added to my packing list for future races.

I set up my transition area and got on my bike for a warm-up spin to run through all the gears and make sure everything was in good working order. It was still dark, and all athletes were using the same road in and out of the transition area for warm-up, so I had to really watch out for runners. I had been relieved to hear that the 3 a.m. water reading resulted in a temperature that would allow wet suits. I made my way partially around the lake for my warm-up, and when I came back my bike was working smoothly and was ready to go. I went back to transition to rack my bike and put on my shoes. All the while, I was looking for my nemesis, but I didn't see her anywhere. For a moment, I thought she might not have made it to the race—and then I realized that she would have to be almost dead for that to happen.

I noticed that the port-o-let lines were getting longer, so I jumped in one of them. When I came out, I did my running drills down the same road I had used for my bike warm-up. When I finished my run, the sun was finally coming up. The forecast was for hot, humid, windy weather. It was looking like a challenging day; still, I couldn't contain my excitement! Before the race, I talked with some of the other racers in my age group to find out their numbers and figure out how I could keep pace throughout the triathlon. My targets for the Lubbock race were 45 minutes for swimming, 2 hours and 45 minutes for biking, and 1 hour and 50 minutes for running.

I ran into the transition area and switched out my running stuff for my wet suit. Everything had to be organized and ready to go in my transition area because the next time I would come back was after the swim, during the race. I made sure everything was ready, downed my energy shot, made my way down to the water to get warmed up, and made my way over to the swim. The water felt cooler than I thought it would be, what with all the concern it would be too warm for wet suits. I calmed my nerves and waded in. I put on my goggles over my cap and my nose plugs in place. I started swimming and it felt good to stretch out my arms and shoulders. The water was a greenish brown with decent visibility, unlike the water I had been swimming in at home—which was murky and full of goose poop.

My coach had told me to warm up effectively, to start slow with long gliding strokes and work into a faster arm cadence to get my heart rate up a bit. I was doing this and making my way back to the shore, wondering why I wasn't seeing any other athletes warming up. I saw my husband waving his arms on the shore to get my attention. I surfaced and heard him yelling for me to get out of the water, motioning that the race start was on the other side of the transition area. Where I was swimming was the swim finish. Oh no! I didn't want to miss the start! Crap! A million things ran through my mind as I made my way to the shore as fast as I could. Talk about getting my heart rate up!

By this time, a couple of race officials saw me and were standing at the shore to help me out of the water and get me over to the start. I exited the water, they took my hand and helped me out, and then my husband and I ran over to where the huge crowd was waiting to start. Oh geez, did I feel like an idiot! How could I have missed seeing all the other athletes warming up for the swim? Duh. Here I was so focused on what I was doing that I missed something huge like that!

The swim start was broken into waves based on age and pro or amateur status, and each was indicated by cap color. I was starting to learn some of the more delicate intricacies of racing, like trying to stay near someone in my age group. My cap was yellow and I joined the rest of the same color caps, hoping no one would notice where I had come from. Everyone was checking their watches and shaking out their arms, trying to shake off the nervousness and anticipation you feel right before the start—which feels like butterflies and sickness.

Suddenly, I saw my nemesis Peyton at the front of our group. Oh, great. Now I had to see if I could stay with her. She looked daunting in her wet suit and cap. The fact that she was at the front while my coach had told me to line up on the outside about three-quarters back told me she was a strong, fast swimmer.

Again, I had tons of thoughts running through my head from all of the training I had done and all of the things I needed to remember—one of which was to start my watch timer when the gun went off so I could have the "gun time" during my race to track how I was doing. At that exact moment, the gun went off and everyone was running into the water and diving below to start swimming. Discombobulated, I followed and pushed the start button on my watch.

The water was full of arms, legs, heads, and thrashing water. The swim start is the worst if you aren't in the front. Everyone is grouped up and basically swimming on top of each other until natural pacing spaces everyone out. Once you get to the buoy to turn, it's a cluster of people again, made worse by low visibility. I was concentrating on swimming in a straight line. There is a whole technique to this in open water versus the swimming pool, since you can't see though the water. It involves "sighting" by lifting your head up slightly to sight the buoy and your line to it during your stroke. I had by no means perfected this or my stroke, so it cost me more time. The good thing about swimming slower than everyone else is you don't have to deal very long with getting beat up by the crowd of swimmers. I thought about speeding up, but wasn't around the last buoy yet, and remembered getting advice not to go above aerobic heart rate during the swim portion of an endurance race. It doesn't make enough of a difference in time and has a detrimental effect on the rest of your race performance. So, I stayed at the same pace, which meant slow and steady. The race director had joked earlier that he swims so slow he has been called a "barge." I thought that was a fitting name for me, too.

As I passed the second buoy, I thought about the next steps in the race and what I needed to do. As I had been taught, I peed in my wet suit as I came into the swim finish. You do this so that you don't have to stop and pee in transition, which takes tons of time. The goal is to be in and out of transition in under two minutes, and there is lots to do: strip off your wet suit (which can be tough getting your feet out and can sometimes result in falling or having to sit down); remove goggles and cap; put on your helmet, socks and shoes, sunglasses, and race number (since you can't wear it in the water), and make sure you have any needed nutrition in your race jersey. For the sake of safety, you have to walk your bike to the end of transition before finally hopping on to start biking.

Karen transitioning from Swimming, Lubbock

As I jumped on my bike, I immediately came to the steep hill I had walked down that morning. Oh shoot, I realized I was in the wrong gear! My bike was in a mid-range gear from my warm up that morning on the flat area.

I struggled to get switched into an easier gear while going up the steep incline and worried that my chain would come off or that I would impede someone behind me and cause an accident. Oh geez, another idiot move! Other athletes were passing me while I was busy looking around—trying to maintain a straight line before I finally shifted into an easier gear, gained momentum, and stood up on my pedals to get up the hill.

Once out on the course, I felt the wind and heat and was happy to be done with the swim. I had not fallen over in transition with dizziness from the swim. My focus became being mindful not to draft off other riders and chasing down my nemesis teammate to pass her decisively. I began to ride efficiently in my aerobars (triathlon bars, or aerobars, include various styles of aerodynamic handlebars for racing bicycles) and I started to pass other athletes. They were few and far between since I had been so far back in the swim. I quickly came to the first aid station and remembered how careful to be, per my coach's advice. I also thought about getting two water bottles: the first one to top off my race water bottle on my handlebars and the second to pour over my head. The volunteers give these to us on the fly. We threw them off to the right once used, all while trying not to get in front of other riders.

Once through, I got back to the business of gaining time and finding my nemesis Peyton. Rider after rider, I searched for the black, white and pink logo of our team but did not see it until the turnaround. I was excited and called out, "Hey, I've got ya!" No response. I said, "Hey, it's Karen." Finally, the woman realized I was talking to her and explained that her sister had loaned her the team jersey. I asked her

Karen Bicycling, Lubbock

where her sister was. Probably nearing the end of the bike course since she was one of the first out of the water in our wave, she replied. Drat! I had been so proud of myself for thinking I had caught her. I had just been too far back in the swim to make up the time. Well, there was probably no catching her, so I decided to continue at a good pace and race as I had planned, letting the chips fall where they may—with Peyton and with my Kona spot.

After I went through the turnaround, the wind kicked up significantly for the ride back. That slowed down lots of riders. Not me. I love the challenge of riding hills, and I saw this as flat hills with wind. I began to break down the barrier between me and other competitors as I announced myself while passing them. You do that to be sure the rider in front knows and so you don't get called for drafting or them for blocking. I overtook a couple of riders who were obviously struggling against the wind, and I called out, "Hey, good job. Keep goin'," when I passed. They looked with surprise, but I liked the feeling of encouraging them. As I passed more riders, I said, "Hey, great job, number so-and-so." This gave me a rhythm and commonality with them, and it took my mind off the challenge of it at the same time. What I found in watching Kona Ironman coverage every year for more than half my life was a spectacle that I couldn't fathom. I loved to watch and try to understand—both for the competitors and for me. Sometimes, I would forget that it would be on and would just happen to catch it. Or my sister would see that it was on and give me a head's up, and we would watch it together and talk, only during the commercial breaks, about what was meaningful to each of us. I was mesmerized by the seemingly super-human feat of it. All at the same time, I felt completely far away from those athletes' experience, yet, I could somehow feel it, taste it, smell it. The Ironman was calling out to me every year when I watched it, and I was operating from fear and staying in my comfort zone in so many parts of my life that it took me 30 years to finally pursue it. At long last, I understood that what appealed to me was the human element. That's why keeping time on everything I did felt empty to me.

I made it back to transition, having made up loads of time. I was still looking for Peyton but had a newfound sense of peace with where I was in the race. The temperature had climbed, and I could see heat radiating off the asphalt as I headed out of transition for the run. I was still nervous, yet I felt good starting the run. My legs felt strong since I had practiced so many bricks to get them used to biking and then running right away. I had stayed cool on the bike, putting water on my head at every aid station, and my nutrition and stomach were doing fine. I was on schedule with taking in gels, liquid nutrition and water. The PowerBar had worked out—although I still wondered at the back of my mind if the Infinit I threw out at my coach's urging would have been okay since I have a pretty strong stomach.

The first part of the run was by the lake in a residential area so there was a lot to look at, which is something I had enjoyed in training and racing. If the scenery is dull, it doesn't hold my attention. Homeowners came out to cheer us on and spray water on us, and the every-mile aid stations had plenty of water, ice, and gels. My coach had told me to run continuously between each aid station at the pace we had laid out, 9- to 9:30-minute miles, which would be easy to time. For 13 miles, that would make my time approximately 127 minutes, which equated to just over two hours. I thought, Okay, this is doable, and settled into that pace. Within the first two miles, the pro-level racers were flying by me in the opposite direction. I was amazed at two things: how skinny they were and how fast they were going at what was the end of their race. I couldn't grasp how they were so skinny and had so much stamina. I was surprised that very few acknowledged my encouragement when I cheered them on as they passed me.

Once past the residential area, I exited the lake park and headed on to the road, down a big hill to the turnaround by the power plant. Pretty flat, but the temperature was boiling and there were no trees in sight. I could see the heat radiating off the asphalt in waves. I loved the heat, but other athletes were wilting. Suddenly, I saw my nemesis Peyton coming my way, looking strong and fast. She smiled and so did I—and that was it. She would beat me decisively, but I justified it by telling myself this was my first Ironman race and she was experienced, so I should go easy on myself. I had to. Otherwise, I never would have gotten through the rest of the race. I saw another woman with whom I had watched Kona coverage at a triathlon event, and she wasn't too far behind my teammate Peyton. She seemed surprised to see me so far back and asked if I was okay. I quickly replied that I'm a slow swimmer and that had put me behind, even though I had made up lots of time on the bike. Then she was gone, too.

After seeing her, I felt a bit dejected, but knew I had to keep putting one foot in front of the other, run my own race, and finish! I realized that I couldn't do anything about what had already happened, but I could keep the pace I had planned and finish strong for myself. There were plenty of people walking or going slower than me at this point. I started doing what I had done when I passed them on the bike, telling them "Good job" or asking where their jersey was from or whatever popped into my head that they could answer quickly. This kept me mentally sharp and alert, which I liked since the thermometer continued to climb. My pace was going decently well until I hit miles 6, 7, and 8. The topography was desolate, brown, and completely uninteresting. I felt bored and wasn't sure how much to keep in the tank to be sure I could finish. I had never done this distance all at once—1.2-mile swim; 56-mile bike; 13 mile run—but I hadn't come all this way not to finish.

I began talking to athletes again. Hearing their stories and exchanging energy took my mind off those boring middle miles. It helped me not miss my iPod that I was used to training with. My pace went from 9:30-minute miles to 10:30, and even one 11-minute mile due to not running the entire mile in between aid stations. At mile 9, I talked to a girl from Texas. She told me she had been running after me, using my pace for the last few miles, and asked why I had slowed. I couldn't answer her and realized how lame I had been in feeling bored. I thanked her for providing clarity and told her I was going to get back to my original pace now. I took off and didn't slow down again. My decision was to only walk at the aid stations, not on the course. I was starting to hone my strategy to make sure to ask the other racers questions after the race to gain knowledge from them.

I had to use the bathroom between miles 11 and 12, and while I did, the woman from Texas caught up to me. When I saw her, she was obviously hurting and limping. Another athlete I had met, a man from Kansas, was helping her and I offered words of encouragement. They both thanked me and told me to return to my pace and finish my race. I agreed, wished them my best, and took off for the finish. As I ran the last mile, I felt strong and had a good pace.

Right before the finish, I noticed a race photographer taking athlete photos. There had been others along the racecourse, too. I wasn't paying much attention to them because I was thinking about the many things I had to remember during the race. I hoped they hadn't snapped any embarrassing pictures. Again, it is just like me to miss something like that! As I ran the last yards, people were cheering, which gave me energy to run faster. In the running-only races I had done before, I always prided myself on finishing with a strong kick, and that natural instinct arose. Before I knew it, I was crossing the finish line, holding my hands up in victory. I felt great having completed my first Ironman race! My stats were swim, 43:04; bike, 3:31:38; run, 2:25:59; total: 6:47:45. I had conquered my limiting beliefs and now had my first official Ironman event under my belt!

The finish line volunteers placed a finisher medal around my neck and gave me an official shirt, which was made of a cool black tech fiber with the race logo in bright colors down one side and the official Ironman logo on the back with the word "finisher." It was official! I was official! My husband took plenty of pictures, including one with me making the Keller Williams Realty hand symbol I had made after my Moab race—the sign language letters "KW". My team manager had organized agents and staff from my Keller Williams office to sign a race event schedule with words of

Karen crossing the Finish Line, Lubbock

encouragement and I wanted to show that I appreciated their support and thought about them during the race.

After I finished the race, I found out the temperature during the run had been 108 degrees! I realized that was why many were having a hard time, but running was my element and heat didn't bother me. For me, the hotter, the better! After I collected all my stuff from transition, we walked with it up the hill to the car. After being in the same clothes since 6 a.m., all I wanted to do was shower, eat, and rest rather than schlep up the hill to the car. My legs and arms ached.

As we drove back to the hotel, my husband told me the pros were already out of the water when he watched my start. They start ahead of the amateur field and complete the swim in roughly 20-30 minutes, then fly by on their bikes. He was surprised at their speed and skinniness compared to amateurs. They were skinny and powerful because as they trained, fat whittled away and their muscles elongated to become more efficient.

Once we arrived at the hotel, we stepped out into the parking lot and the asphalt was so hot it was melting and making the bottoms of our shoes sticky. We carried all our stuff inside and the cold temperature from the air conditioning gave me some relief from the heat. I couldn't wait to hit the shower. I grabbed any food I could find as I made my way to the bathroom. I turned the shower on and stepped in. As I washed, I could feel the sunburn marks and the abrasions from the friction of my arms pumping during the run and the seat abrasions from cycling. I was glad that I wasn't chafed from the wet suit since that was a common complaint from other athletes. Thankfully, I always used copious amounts of the anti-chafe Bodyglide product so everything moved easily.

There was an athlete dinner and awards, but that wasn't until 7 that night and I was starving. I told my husband I wanted ice cream and we found a Cold Stone Creamery. I had this uneasy feeling like my stomach was concave and that nothing I ate, no matter how much, would fill it up. This was the first time I had ever experienced that. I ordered a large chocolate dipped waffle cone with two scoops of ice cream, brownies, chocolate fudge, and sprinkles. I was never able to eat that much before, but I had a big appetite and wanted to treat myself for finishing the race. It was like a second stomach opened up and I wasn't capable of getting full. Looking back, I know that I was facing a significant calorie deficit from the day even though I had followed my fuel plan every twenty minutes as my coach had instructed. My body was doing anything it could to catch up. This was a weird experience for me because normally my stomach could only take so much food in one sitting before I felt full, but this was truly an exception. I remembered that one of the pros I talked to said that no matter how you fuel during the race, your body will be behind in the calorie consumption needed compared to the expenditure during the race. It made sense that my body was trying to catch up.

We headed back to the hotel and I rested a while before it was finally time for the awards dinner. My body wanted to stay in bed, but I knew I would regret it if I didn't go. Besides, I didn't want to miss out on the festivities of the evening since I had earned my spot there. The room was buzzing when we walked in, so crowded it was hard to move and everyone with overflowing plates. Tables of food lined the side of the room with overflowing vats of rice, potatoes, vegetables, rolls, and more. We loaded up and found a seat with the Ironman triathlete I'd met at the pre-race meeting. He said he'd had a good day, with cramping problems because of the heat and ended up with a slower time than he would need to grab a Kona spot. I felt the same, without the cramping. My swim had been slower than I'd hoped to do, and that threw the total time off. I was concerned that I didn't have a time fast enough to grab a spot. I looked for Peyton, hoping that she wasn't coming to the awards and wouldn't stand in my way of getting a spot in Kona.

While the room was whirling with conversation and good cheer, the race director took the stage and talked about the day. Everything had gone smoothly and the weather wasn't the worst or the best compared to recent years. The room quieted, everyone sat in anticipation and could sense the tension in the room as they awaited the news. He explained they would begin with the pro awards, move on to the youngest age groups, and then to the oldest. Everyone cheered when he announced that they would have Kona and Las Vegas spots the following year and I knew that he was saying this to put our minds at ease since many wouldn't end up with a spot for the races this year.

As I glanced around the room and wondered whether or not I would even want to return to Lubbock and try again if I didn't get a spot, I questioned whether I was being presumptuous and unrealistic to expect to get a spot at my first race. Many people had been trying for years. Many athletes decide that they want to not only complete an Ironman, but find their way to qualifying for the World Championships, which is very difficult to do. It becomes their life's work to realize their dream, and many work at it for ten years or more. I saw a story about a man who completed 28 Ironman races to get there! I reminded myself that whatever was supposed to happen would happen. If I got a spot there in whatever way, I would go to Kona.

They began with the pro women and when the top three athletes' names and times were announced, I realized how fast they were. They had finished in half the time it took me. They approached the stage and the director asked if they wanted to claim their spots to Kona or Las Vegas. I sat there thinking, who in their right mind would say no to Kona? I didn't understand it, but it happened. One of the pros said no and rolled the spot down to the next finisher. I asked my new Ironman friend why the person wouldn't take their spot and he explained that it probably involved her training and that she probably didn't want to go to Kona until she could have her best performance, kind of like a fine seasoning.

The process continued with the male pros, and then the age groups began with the youngest males—including Drew Scott, who finished first in his group. Drew made his way to the stage. When the race director asked him if he wanted to take his spot for Kona, he took the microphone and said, "Dad, can you give me the money to take the Kona spot?" The crowd broke into wild laughter. I thought of how lucky he was to be coached by the legendary Dave Scott, have won his first race, and have the opportunity to go to Kona. I so wanted to be him in that moment! His dad nodded his head and said yes, then got out his checkbook to pay for his son's spot for Kona.

They continued with the rest of the age groups, and a couple of other athletes didn't take their Kona spots. My friend told me that sometimes the decision to pass on Kona is an economic one since it is costly to go. When they got to my age group, I straightened up and listened, looking intently at the speaker. I had placed 34th and the chances of my getting a roll-down spot were nearly impossible. Then, my nightmare began. My nemesis Peyton finished fifth and a rolling spot went to her. The others sitting at her table stood and cheered for her. All I could think about was how she didn't deserve to go because of her bad attitude.

Once they got to the last age group, I saw the lady and her husband who had had been buying soda and moon pies in the convenience store when I arrived in Lubbock. They both got qualifying spots and I thought how much I wanted to be like them when I got to their age. They didn't seem to have a care in the world and there were not many other people in their age group. I was happy for them and acknowledged that if they had been at it this long, they deserved their spots. It was a good experience and I knew I had my first official Ironman race under my belt.

As we drove back to Colorado, I thought about what I would say to my agents. They were all rooting for me and praying that I qualified for Kona. I didn't want to disappoint them, and I felt a weight on my shoulders. I realized that though I didn't qualify at Lubbock, nothing would stop me from getting there. That's exactly what I would share with them. I decided to focus on how I had thought of them throughout the race. They were each with me in spirit, and I was overwhelmed with gratitude for their love and support. It was one of the things that held me up and helped me conquer the beliefs that limited me. It had carried me through my training and the race. I posted pictures and messages from the race, and when I returned they were even more supportive than when I'd left. I knew I was encircled by an amazing group of people.

The Story of My Nemesis

The assistant for my real estate team, Cindy, knew a woman who was training for Kona, and she arranged a time we could all get together. She would introduce the two of us at dinner so I could ask her friend questions about Kona. This friend had been there before and wanted to go back to improve on her time. As it turned out, she also was a coach and worked within Gretchen's organization.

Cindy and I got to the restaurant and made small talk as we waited for her friend—who, to my mind, could just as well have been the Queen of England. Then she strutted into the restaurant talking on the phone. She had a ball cap pulled over her wet, chlorinated hair and wore skin tight jeans that made her look like a short, stocky guy. Cindy and I had come from work so we were both dressed up. The other woman started to speak with Cindy and ignored me entirely.

After Cindy introduced her to me, she immediately asked if I had a coach. I wondered how she could not know that her own boss was my coach, and it left me feeling uneasy.

When she finished catching up with Cindy about their kids' activities, she asked me, "So you want to go to Kona, huh?" I replied with a joyful yes, and asked her to tell me what it was like—what it feels like, sounds like, everything. The conversation we had was not quite what I anticipated. In fact, it made me feel sick. She looked straight into my eyes and said Kona was a "suffer-fest" — it was all about how much you were willing to suffer. I didn't really understand and looked perplexed.

She explained that Kona is a hot, windy, long race, and that you push yourself beyond all limits. Each stroke, each pedal, and each step becomes part of a battle against everyone else in the Ironman. She told me that during the race, athletes are hot and smelly. In some cases, they are known to urinate while in the bike leg by leaning their derrière off to one side. This is affectionately known as "peeing off the bike." I was definitely taken aback and a little disgusted as she explained how urine gets into your shoes, you shouldn't wear white because urine shows, and it might land on your close competitor and slow them down. I thought, this was not the conversation I was expecting to have. She said she had used the peeing tactic against her competitors. She said she hoped I wouldn't be menstruating because that was just a pain to deal with on race day during transition. She said I'd end up with blood running down my legs, too, so make sure I had a dark colored race kit. I was horrified, especially as she went on to say that if you have stomach problems you'll have diarrhea, too, and will end up doing the "Ironman shuffle" on the way to the finish line. The Ironman Shuffle is when you pinch your behind together to prevent fecal matter dripping down your backside causing you to shuffle instead of run.

I wasn't sure if she was trying to scare me off from pursuing Kona or if this was a realistic introduction to what Kona was going to be like. I'd never had any of those issues during any other race, and I wondered what she was eating prior to and during the Ironman. I convinced myself that I would never pee off my bike. She told me I needed to be willing to do anything to get to Kona and be able to perform there. I started to question myself, wondering if I had what it took to get there because I was disgusted at the mere prospect of doing some of the things she described.

She told me the training leading up to the race and the race itself were both exhausting. When I asked about the crowds, the pageantry, the history and the icons, she blew my questions off. I thought that there was no way she deserved to return to Kona because she lacked respect for the place, the race, and the people. I knew she was looking at her experience as one of suffering and pain.

She ended up being my nemesis and my competition in qualifying for a slot in Kona. At the same time, my coach was training her, so she was my team member in a sense. As I mentioned, I called her "Peyton."

Her words and the meaning behind them frightened me. I wondered if I had what it took to suffer. No one had ever put it in such terms before. I had trained and raced, and I never equated the difficult situations in my life to suffering. She continued talking about her personal problems, and hearing her talk was making me sick. I excused myself and went into the bathroom to splash water on my face and clear my head.

When I returned to the table, she shifted gears and started telling me why she should coach me, knowing I had already hired her boss. I was confused and angry at the suggestion and put my anger into eating. I started consuming my dinner like a ravenous animal so I could get away from her toxic monologue. She was an unbelievable mess, and when dinner was over I thanked her, and Cindy and left the restaurant.

On the drive home, I called Crystal to tell her what had happened and to try and calm myself down. Crystal reminded me about all that I had been through and prevailed over. She told me that the woman was probably insecure, and she was also my competition. She might have been trying to scare me out of competing. Everything Crystal said clicked, and I took comfort in her words. I really never wanted to see that woman again, but I knew I would end up seeing her at some of our team events. So, I made a promise to myself not to let her drama influence me and to keep her at a healthy distance.

The benefit of meeting her was that it made me really look at how I needed to become mentally and physically tough. I had gone into my training for Kona thinking it was almost entirely physical and I already possessed the mental toughness I would need. I realized I had a lot to learn. I began to read books to help me understand the mental game of competing, and I read articles in triathlon magazines by the top pros. I learned my subconscious mind and the beliefs it held about my abilities were driving my actions, stopping progression in swimming and running. From this, I learned how to conquer limiting beliefs: I made a list of all of the things I was saying—to myself and others—that were keeping me from progressing. Topping the list was, I am not a great swimmer, I am not a fast runner. Beside each item, I wrote the exact opposite, positive phrase or belief. I put on a rubber bracelet to serve as a reminder. When the negative thoughts came to mine, I snapped the bracelet on my wrist (ouch!). To move it to the opposite meaning, I said out loud, "I AM A GREAT SWIMMER! I AM A FAST RUNNER!" (Yes, I got some laughs and weird looks when I did this in public!) I was re-wiring my subconscious, habitual, limiting-belief thoughts with new, unlimited, empowering ones that would drive different actions and cause me to improve. It felt contrived at first, but it became automatic very quickly. My swimming and running improved, and I then applied it to other parts of my life where negative beliefs and thoughts were limiting me in my life. It worked there, too.

Because of this encounter with my nemesis—someone who scared me and who held attitudes I didn't agree with—I became stronger and began to conquer my own limiting beliefs. Rather than focus on her, I focused on me and how I could use this experience to get better and achieve my dreams.

Chapter 9

Second Attempt at Earning a Kona Qualifying Spot

The Boulder Half Ironman was in August 2011. The Friday before the race, I traveled north the hour or so to Boulder to pick up my athlete packet. I was happy to finally be able to shop for official Ironman merchandise! The Boulder race, I was told, would have a super-sized tent with plenty of great product. It was a pretty, hot summer day, and I enjoyed the drive up. I arrived after work, and it was already crowded. I wanted to hurry and get my athlete packet and spend quality time shopping.

I have always enjoyed Boulder. It is a mountain town nestled in the foothills of the Rocky Mountains, a short drive from my home. It normally has a moderate climate, but the day of the Boulder Half Ironman was predicted to be a scorcher, with temperatures to climb up to 96 degrees F.

Collecting my packet went smoothly, and I made my way to the Ironman tent. My friends were right: it was a double-sized tent filled to the brim with shirts, shorts, race gear, books, and DVDs—everything you could imagine and more. When my sister Ruby and best friend Crystal entered the tent with me, we were all amazed to see everything. It seemed like a magical place. The first thing I found was a hard-back book documenting every Kona World Championship event of the last 30 years, beginning with the very first one. It had a ton of color photos and stories I was familiar with. I began reading with intense focus.

My emotions churned as I as gazed at images of my icons from the previous 30 years of the race, and, as I turned the pages, I started sobbing. To believe that I could go and compete in the same race they had competed in really moved me. I couldn't stop looking at the book and crying. Finally, I looked up at my sister. From across the display table, she looked back and saw my emotion. I held up the book to show her. Immediately, she understood. Ruby is athletic, just like me. I saw her playing sports early in my life and I think that rubbed off on me. She played basketball, volleyball, fast pitch softball; she went skiing, biking, and running. She taught me how to mountain bike. In every instance of my life, my sister had led by example, and I followed. Ruby is also an eternal optimist and has a total can-do attitude. She roots for the under-dog and will sacrifice anything to help someone else.

I think part of the reason my sister immediately understood my need to be true to myself regarding Kona is that she fought on a very personal level to be true to herself. She fought ignorance disguised as cruelty, fought fear disguised as prejudice. Ruby is gay and has traveled a long road to be who she is. She tried to go the traditional route in middle and high school, dating guys and trying to conform to what she felt pressured to be by society. Then, she just couldn't pretend anymore. To alleviate her pain, she spent ten years self-medicating with drugs and worked very short-term menial labor jobs. After that, she decided to serve her country and completed the rigorous work involved in becoming a member of the Marine Corps—only to be discharged when they found out she was gay. It was yet another painful experience of not being accepted for who she was. She returned home, and formally told us she was gay. We loved her more than ever. Our mom said she always knew Ruby was gay from when she was a baby. I think I knew, too.

Once Ruby came out to us, she seemed to flourish. Being accepted for who you are is so often the catalyst for reaching your potential—and for sparking the desire to reach for it! For Ruby, this included going back to school and earning her degree. She studied psychology, as well as women's studies, traveling to Africa as a part of her curriculum. My sister very much wanted to help people and make a difference in the world. She continues today, striving to be the best she can while serving her community. She has devoted her entire professional career to working at a homeless shelter.

As I held up the book to show Ruby, she made her way over to me. We leafed through it together and she became choked up, as well. Then Crystal made her way over and when I showed her the book I said, "See, this is what Ironman means to me." She got it. I know she understood it long before that. This was merely the evidence, the three-dimensional proof I could use to show her. The three of us hugged and went our separate ways to look at other merchandise—and I would not let that book go. I considered it mine and carried it the whole time until I was ready to pay for my purchases.

I bought some other items and Crystal snuck around and bought me a short sleeve t-shirt with "Ironman in training 2012" printed across the front. The word Ironman was in pink, one of my favorite colors. She surprised me with it that weekend and I was proud to wear it, feeling like I finally had something that was officially Ironman, and I could announce to the world what I was doing. It felt like a source of strength to me and I so loved her for getting it for me.

Ironman stickers act as a code of honor among triathletes. I really wanted Kona Ironman stickers because their presence would represent the pursuit of my dream. They only sell them at races, so they are consequently coveted and protected. I even asked the athletes I knew who had been there to give me one for visualization, and they all declined. They told me I needed to earn it—only then could I buy and display one. I was excited that here at my first Ironman race in Boulder in 2011, I could get a sticker with the Ironman logo. I bought a clear cling for my window so that I could look at it every day for inspiration and as a reminder of my dream and progress. I knew I would be an Ironman someday, and this was the visual I needed to get me there.

The pre-race athlete meeting was more of a festival with food, speakers, and Ironman gear. I noticed athletes wearing full length socks on this hot day. I couldn't figure out what that meant, especially when some of them were bright colors worn with shorts or skorts. Someone explained they were compression socks that push the blood back up your legs. The theory is that it helps with faster muscle recovery. I blurted, "Well, I'll never wear those. They look ridiculous!" Little did I know it would be only a short time before I was wearing them regularly, and being similarly judged for it, too!

One of the pros in this race was Andy Potts, whom I had always thought highly of. He was a super-fast swimmer—not to mention good looking. I happened to have a red cap with me and I waited in line for 15 minutes to have him sign it. He was nice and completely unassuming. He asked about this race and I told him my goal. He said he had the same one. He hoped we would see each other in Kona that year, and that made me feel like we had something in common. Maybe we could both get there.

The Ironman in Colorado was a long anticipated event, especially for the triathletes in the area. Racing on my own turf could work to my advantage, because I was accustomed to the elevation and the hills. I was excited, especially since Crystal, Ruby, and the agents from my office would be able to come to the race with me. I had focused my training on improving my running time and my technique and speed in swimming. I completed several training rides with my coach to improve my cycling methods. I knew that if I did not try to better myself in all three disciplines, one or two would slip. I did not want to make a mistake that would interfere with my journey to Kona.

Race day was cloudy, chilly, and dewy. Crystal got up to drive with me at 4:30 in the morning, and it was still nighttime when we met up with Ruby in Boulder. I thought they were both troopers to get up so early to help me on their weekends. Crystal was a night owl who would wake at 7 or 8 in the morning and go to bed around midnight or 2 a.m. The fact that she got up to be at my house at 4:30 a.m. was not just a Herculean effort; it was an example of her immeasurable love and support.

Once in Boulder, we transferred all the gear to the transition area. Having a half-Ironman under my belt, I felt less scared than at Lubbock. But here I had agents, tri-team, coaches, family and friends who had all come out to watch me, and I felt some pressure. I didn't want to let them down, and I wanted my performance in the race to show that all their encouragement and effort during my training had made a difference. I wanted them all, especially my coach Gretchen, to see my progress. I was more excited than at the previous race and less fearful (about 25 percent fear to 75 percent excitement!) but the butterflies were always there—especially thinking about the swim start. There were a lot of people in one area, I was a fearful swimmer, and I would start breathing heavy at the start until I got into a rhythm. This was also when I'd start swimming by myself because the pack was swimming far faster than me and had left me behind. Having said this, I was still totally up for a great race day.

My experience had taught me to arrive early. There were always unforeseen problems, and that morning would be no exception. As we made our way from the car to the transition area, I lost the straw for my handlebar bike race bottle. This left me with no way to drink water on the fly. Disposable water bottles would only slow me down and, if they didn't have caps, make a mess for me and the other racers. I looked everywhere I could think of and re-checked everything in my bags and the car. The straw was simply gone and I didn't have a backup. We asked some of the other athletes in the transition area if they had an extra, but no one did. I called my coach, but she would not be getting to the race until after I started and wouldn't be able to enter the athlete-only transition area. As I got the rest of my stuff ready so I could start warming up, but I worried about how the race would go if I didn't have the stupid straw.

Suddenly, Crystal had the idea to use a Starbucks straw since they had a longer length that might work in the bottle. All I could think of was what a genius she was to think of it as she went to the car to search for the nearest Starbucks. Ruby stayed behind to help me get warmed up. I saw several friends I had come to know through mountain biking, road biking, and triathlons. They were all supportive and wished me the best of luck on my quest for Kona. I felt physically and mentally prepared for the race. I was ready to get my spot! I did my bike warm-up on the residential streets around the Boulder reservoir where

I often trained and everything felt familiar. My nerves from the loss of the straw seemed to melt away. I did my warm-up run in the other direction, where I had run other races and boated. I felt like I was at home and in my element.

Then Crystal came running up, Starbucks straw in hand, and gave it to me over the fence since I was in the transition area just for athletes. I hugged her over the fence and thanked her. I knew that the straw would be just the ticket and thanked God that she had thought of it.

At the beach, the buoys were so far out that I could hardly see them. The loop looked daunting. I reminded myself I could accomplish anything I set my mind to and prayed that God would give me strength. I pulled my wet suit on and made sure all my gear was laid out properly in the transition area. I had eaten my energy gel twenty minutes before. Everything was ready to go. I grabbed my goggles, cap, and nose plug and met Ruby and Crystal down at the water to warm up before the race start. I had trouble getting my goggles to seal. Ruby helped me make sure my cap was out of the way so my goggles were squarely on my face. I went back out to test them and almost

Karen, Boulder Half IM

missed the start for my swim wave. Luckily, Crystal and Ruby had my back and whistled at me as I got out of the water. When I looked up, they yelled and motioned for me to run over to my group, which was lined up waiting for the sound of the starting gun. I felt like a gazelle as I ran toward them and lined up in the back—just as the starting gun sounded. I was on the side of the pack where I liked to be positioned.

The swim went well, though I collided with other swimmers a few times. It rattled me, but I kept on going. I exited the water and ran up the ramp to transition and heard the loving, familiar voices of the important people in my life, which gave me the push I needed to run faster. Transition went smoothly, and I was soon out on my bike, doing the already-familiar loop. I was going fast and things were going well.

The bike course consisted of two loops. I sped out of Boulder Reservoir Park, onto the course going west after seeing Ruby and Crystal cheer me on. There wasn't much wind and it was getting warmer, but not too hot. I began passing riders frequently. I stayed on top of my nutrition and maintained a fast pace. From going through the course with my coach, I knew where I could accelerate and where I should be more careful. As I finished my first loop, I realized I was faster than I had told Ruby and Crystal I would be, which meant they wouldn't be in position to see me when I came by. I would miss seeing them, but I was happy to be faster than my prediction for the first time. As I rounded the corner, completing the loop, I thought, Now, I just need to negative split the second loop. (Negative split is where the second half of the race is faster than the first.) I knew it was a fine line between pushing harder for a faster second loop and having something left for the run. I decided to go as fast on the bike as on my first loop, and identified three areas where I could be a bit faster without taking too much strength.

It was then, while I was concentrating on keeping my pedal cadence high, that I noticed someone drafting off of me. I heard them breathing heavy behind me and then saw their shadow. I thought they would call out a pass, but they never did. I became annoyed because they were gaining advantage off my strong bike leg. I turned around to tell them off and realized I was on a public road that had not been closed off for the race and the person "drafting" off me was a recreational cyclist out for a fun ride. It was just like me to get all intense about something without realizing that the person behind me was just having fun! I laughed at myself after seeing the man's surprised face when I turned around and looked at him so intensely.

I continued the rest of the loop and about halfway through, began to see Kathy, a girl I had been playing "leapfrog" with most of the course. She and I seemed to be of the same speed and strength on the bike, which is why we kept jostling for position. I accelerated past her on the hills, and she passed me on the descents. With less than 5 miles to go, I struck up a conversation, asking her where she was from. She told me Highlands Ranch, which is a suburb of Denver I rode through all the time, and where my coach, bike mechanic, and lots of friends lived. I told her we should probably train together since we were of similar riding strength and she agreed. We exchanged names and agreed to connect on Facebook.

With that, I passed her for the last time and headed into the final leg, down the road to the reservoir and transition area. Crystal and Ruby realized they had missed me and were walking the mile back to the transition area when I raced by, calling out to them. Their backs were toward me and by the time they turned around, I passed them. They cheered me on, and I yelled that I had the fastest bike time ever, crushing my goal. I felt electrified to share it with them and reported that the Starbucks straw had worked beautifully.

When I entered transition, I could feel the heat climbing and knew the run would be hot, confirming my plan to start filling my run hat with ice as soon as possible. (Triathletes use ice on various parts of their bodies to avoid heat exhaustion). The run was on dirt roads and paths that had seen a lot of hot dry weather recently, and it was dusty. Many people were struggling and starting to walk. The running route included two loops. Having done this route before, I knew the toughest part for me would be the long, boring straightaway from the park behind the reservoir to the front of it. There were things to look at, but the stretch seemed to last forever and was totally open with no trees for shade.

My coach and team were at the race to support several team athletes competing. The coaches were taking pictures from the team tent and I was excited to run by them the first time at the close of the first loop. My coach said I looked strong and to pour on the speed in the second loop. My cadence picked up as I ran by her, but after I got out of the park and onto the hot dirt road going uphill, my speed and strength began to fade. I saw athletes "hitting the wall" and sitting down on the side of the road. I couldn't bring myself to look at their faces, for fear their disease of giving in would plague me. I said a prayer for each one as I went by, hoping they would find the strength to continue.

I knew I could finish the race; I didn't know how much to push my speed. I began talking to a few people, which gave me a bit of energy. But I still grew bored during those middle miles, and it showed in my pace. I began drinking cola at every other water station, hoping it would sharpen me up. I hadn't tried it before, and I hoped it would be okay in my stomach. I figured I'd better try it now and know whether I could use cola in Kona, because they would have it there. I remembered a former pro friend telling me they called it "black gold" because the sugar and caffeine were so effective at charging you up with no stomach upset. I thought, if it worked for the pros, it would probably help me.

At mile 11, I fell in with a group of runners and we discussed racing and getting to Kona. By this time I was sore, hot, chafed, and getting stiff from the day's events. It hurt to run, but not excruciatingly. Upon hearing my goal, one girl said to me, "Well, girl, run and get your spot!" That lit the fire in me to speed my way to the finish. The final leg into the finish was down a hill on pavement, so I turned on my usual kick and powered through. I saw my coach and other athletes from our team cheering for me and I ran faster, pumping my arms to counter my legs and keep my balance so I could go faster. I remembered my coach telling me I should feel like puking at the end just to be sure I had put in all of my effort. I ran through the finish line, and there were Crystal and Ruby waiting for me.

Once the volunteer grabbed my timing chip, I made my way over to hug them. I looked at my watch and the race clock and knew I was under six hours, which meant I had knocked almost an hour off my Lubbock time! I thought surely that time was fast enough for a qualifying spot. I stretched and got food and water at the athlete tent, then went over to the team tent to see how the others had done. My coach gave me a "Good job" and asked if I puked; when I said no, she seemed disappointed. She asked if I could have gone faster, and I said I wanted to be sure to finish, but my time was so much faster than Lubbock. She didn't say anything to that. I asked how the other athletes had done. Two had done well and two had issues, either stomach or muscular, and dropped out of the race. My nemesis wasn't there and I was thankful for that, as I felt like no one overshadowed me that day. My stats: swim, 47:20; bike, 2:54:55; run, 2:03:58.

After my post-race routine, I found the official timing tent to check out my finishing position against the rest of my age group. I was astounded to see the fast times in my age group. The top finisher was almost an hour faster than me! I had been so sure I was going to be fast enough to get a spot. Now I was worried the same thing would happen to me as had in Lubbock, and I wouldn't get a roll down. I think I was in 16th place, and I knew there wouldn't be a roll-down that far. Feeling dejected, I didn't even stay for the awards or roll-down ceremonies. I went on home with Crystal and Ruby who continued to tell me not to worry, that I would still get to Kona. They offered me encouragement and the reassurance that I had done a great job that day. God love them!

Chapter 10

Cambridge, MD, Half Ironman

My plan was to compete in the August 2012 Louisville, KY full Ironman to earn a qualifying spot to Kona. Then in April 2012, I found out I had won a spot through the lottery. I was ecstatic that I was going to compete in Kona. What was required now was to validate that spot by completing a half or full Ironman. I chose the Cambridge, MD half Ironman for this in June of 2012. I was anxious to show I was capable and ready to compete in the Kona Ironman World Championships. I had been willing to do everything it took to get here and this would be the culmination of that demonstration! I had to get to Cambridge first!

I didn't know how early to make lodging arrangements for the June 2012 Cambridge Half Ironman, and waited until four months before the race. At least, that was what I told myself when I couldn't find anywhere to stay! Truth be told, I'd waited too long to make my plans for this Kona Qualifier Race. In February and March, I started looking around on the lodging sites partnered with Ironman, and everything was already booked. I started searching online and ended up calling every motel and hotel near the race start—I even got on two waiting lists for smoking rooms! At that point, I was truly desperate and starting to get frustrated.

At Keller Williams, my agents started asking me for updates about when and where my upcoming race was and how my training was going. One Sunday evening, I was officially starting to panic, and that night I prayed to God to help me figure out what I was supposed to do. A deep sense of calm came over me. I knew everything would be okay for the race. The next morning, I went into the office and an agent, one of the sweetest people on the face of the earth, asked me if I had a place to stay at the race, because her sister lived there. I was amazed, but not surprised, as it seemed as though God had it all taken care of.

It took a week for my agent to connect her sister and me, and then we found that she lived too far from the race location. Even though she would have gladly put me up during the race, the drive was way too long to consider. She could hear the panic in my voice, so she offered to put the word out among her active, athletic friends. She also suggested I check vacation rentals and bed and breakfast sites. I hadn't even thought of those!

I went back online, searching for bed and breakfasts first. I saw one called Victoria Gardens Inn. It looked beautiful, so I called and left a voicemail inquiring about the dates I needed for the race. I called two more places, neither of which had openings. It was time for me to go out for my bike ride. Though I should have been worried, I wasn't. I knew it would be okay. God would put me where I was supposed to be. When I returned from my bike ride, a British woman had left two voice messages. She said she didn't have any room at her B&B and would check with other owners to see if they had anything. Her next message said one of the owners had an opening and she gave me their contact information.

Before I could call the owner, the British woman called back. She introduced herself as Lynette, the owner of the Victoria Gardens Inn. She asked if I was coming to town for the Ironman race and said the race was why everything was full. In her calls to other area owners, she had found an available one-bedroom and had called on my behalf to see if she could reserve it. During our conversation, it dawned on her that the room was better suited to a couple than to me. Crystal was accompanying me to this race. She went on to work it out by sending her clients over to the other establishment to make room for Crystal and me at her inn. I was absolutely speechless that this stranger had spent her afternoon switching her clients over to another property just to help me out. I couldn't find the words to thank her.

She went on to tell me I could call her with any more questions that came up about the area and she would forward any information she came across to me. I thanked God right then for creating that connection with Lynette. When I shared the story with Crystal, she was equally amazed by Lynette's extraordinary kindness and, like me, couldn't wait to meet her.

This kindness continued from Lynette. As the day of our departure grew near, I asked her logistical questions about how we would get into her house when we arrived. She explained that the front door would be unlocked, and she would wait up. I asked her repeatedly if she was sure—by the time we landed, picked up the rental car and drove to her house, it would be 1 a.m. She assured me this was the way she did things. I was touched by how unequivocally generous she was.

Lynette gave us the attic suite with our own bathroom, big living room, and big bedroom. She told us other race athletes were staying there and we would see them the next day. Lynette's house was an hour outside of Washington, D.C., and Crystal and I had sightseeing plans for between my daily workouts. Every morning, Lynette had a gourmet breakfast ready for us with the best espresso coffee ever. We had great conversations with her about her story, our stories, and the gorgeous area, which was right on the water. I would do a quick workout, shower, and then run errands and see the sights with Crystal. We were busy, and it ended up being a bit much for me, and I was exhausted by the time the race came.

The day before the race, Lynette told us I should meet two gentlemen who were staying that night. I racked my brain over who they could be and why Lynette would suggest I meet them. When I went to the athlete pre-race meeting, I had gotten autographs and had my picture taken with Craig Alexander, Mirinda

Carfrae, and a few others. I asked Lynette if it was any of them. She said no, but, of course, she couldn't divulge who the other guests were.

Crystal helped me make final preparations for race day, check my gear, run errands, and prepare race day food. Lynette answered a knock at the door, ushered in a man with salt-and-pepper hair and introduced him as Andy. I didn't recognize him at first and asked him what he did for a living. He shifted the focus and started asking me about my background. After answering all of his questions about my history as a triathlete and what I was looking to do, he explained that he was the new CEO of the World Triathlon Corporation! I just about died from shock as those words sank in. Lynette was so utterly casual about introducing me and here was the man who was responsible for keeping in place the lottery system that had provided the path for me to realize my lifelong dream of competing in Kona. I almost fell to my knees.

He asked how many years I had been trying and entering the lottery. When I told him, he immediately calculated my odds as 500 to 1 to get a spot in my second year of trying. I told him I knew God had put my name on that list, and it didn't matter what the odds were. Andy was a nice man and excused himself to meet his family for dinner. He was racing the next day, as well.

The other person Lynette wanted me to meet turned out to be Rob Ulrich, head of USA Triathlon. Lynette was just as casual about introducing him, and I began to wonder who else she knew. Her house was in such a prime location; I thought for sure she had pro athletes stay there. But when I pressed her, she was coy and wouldn't admit to anyone specifically. What a great lady!

While staying there, I met a woman named Tyla who was from Detroit and who was there to get a Kona spot as well. Tyla was ultra-fit and we had the same last name. She had a fancy bike with electronic shifting and was more driven than any other triathlete I had met to date—which was amazing, because I had met many uber-driven athletes. She had recently broken her wrist and was still going to race! Unbelievable. There was another competitor staying in Lynette's house, an east coast woman older than I who had finished many Ironman distance races. Because of our different schedules, I didn't see her until after the race.

At the athlete pre-race meeting, a panel of several pro athletes took audience questions. The pros on the panel included Craig Alexander, Mirinda Carfrae, and Meredith Kessler. Cambridge was a training race for all of them, and it made me proud to think that I would be racing the same course as these world-renowned triathletes. They were gracious with their time in answering a great many questions, especially since most of the questions repeated. I could tell they were careful not to divulge any true details of their training; they gave general answers unless the response included a product from one of their sponsors. I understood the position they were in and respected them for what they were doing to get what they wanted, which was to make a living racing professionally. I knew they didn't live a life of opulence, and they were the epitome of hard work.

They agreed to sign autographs and take pictures with fans, so as proof that my dream was coming to fruition, I stepped up to have the hat my friend Karen got me from the World Championships the year before signed by them. Crowie and Rinni (nicknames for Craig Alexander and Mirinda Carfrae), my two favorite pros, signed my hat. They were kind and accommodating, and they looked at me differently when I mentioned the name Brandon del Campo, a friend who lived in Boulder and trained with them. It was as though the veil of the general public came down. They asked how I knew him and what my goals were. For a brief moment, I felt like I belonged with them. Even though we had different paths, we shared the common goal of getting to Kona.

I went back to Lynette's to eat dinner. It was only 4 or 5 p.m. but I needed to be sure my food could completely digest before I went to bed at eight o'clock. I planned to get up at 3:30 a.m. I always felt like a grandma the night before races because I ate dinner like a late lunch, went to bed like a baby, and rose like an old person. My friends were merciless as they teased me over my pre-race routine.

Lynette chatted with Crystal and me out in her beautiful garden. She asked me about my goals for the next day and she divulged some of her personal life and past. She and Crystal hit it off famously and had many things in common. They began chatting about world travels, places they'd visited in common, and a variety of other topics. I was happy listening to them and realized how much they knew about a wealth of subjects. I felt like I only knew two subjects really well: triathlon and real estate. Those two areas seemed to consume all my time, which always made me wonder how others had time to stay current on events, politics and the like. I guess when all your time isn't spent training, recovering, researching, and preparing for races, it amounts to the time one needs to know about other things. Those other things bored me. Although they were nice to know, I never felt like I could make a difference in any of them. In real estate and triathlon, I could have an impact. This was how I had been my entire life, and I was happy with it. Just recognizing this difference between myself and others made me feel at peace.

I bade both of them good night and went off to bed. They were going to stay up talking for a while, and Crystal gave me "the nod" that she knew the schedule for the next day and I could count on her. I went up to our room and went through everything one final time to make sure I was ready for the wee hours the next day. I read an encouraging note from one of my best friends for the race the next day. I could hear his voice as I read, and his words made me feel strong and supported. I had been getting text and Facebook messages from other friends who knew I was preparing for my race. They made me feel loved despite my usual nervousness the night before a big race. I turned off the light, knowing it would be quite some time before I could shut my brain off and sleep. So goes the journey before each race, and it never changed. There wasn't one time when I could turn off the light and fall right to sleep.

The morning of the race, I got up early to prepare and ate breakfast at 3:45 a.m. Many others in the house waited until 4:30 a.m. I liked the idea of being well prepared, and the race would start at 8 a.m. In other races, I'd felt hungry by the start of the race or at the end of the swim, so I wanted to be sure I ate enough breakfast this time. I had three-quarters of a green smoothie, two hard-boiled eggs, and a piece of cinnamon toast. It seemed like I was forcing down every bite and sip, and I was quickly full. I had a couple gulps of my favorite Rockstar to get me going and then went upstairs to begin getting dressed in my race kit. This involved putting Bodyglide balm all over to avoid chafing in the wet suit and race kit. Since the race lasts hours in the hot sun, with sweat and seawater and tap water, it is important for the Bodyglide to last. I layered on sunscreen and deodorant, even though it seemed like an exercise in futility since I would be body marked at the transition area. I pulled on my race kit and it felt good. It felt like my fighting armor or a superhero cape. Either way, it solidified the moment, and I knew I was ready to race.

I started gathering up gear to stage on the porch of the house, preparing to walk over to the transition area; that's how close we were to it. Crystal helped me make sure I had everything I needed, including the Starbucks straws that had become my backup water bottle straws. She was prepping for the long day ahead of her, which would include waiting in the blazing sun for the two times she would see me, followed by more waiting until the finish. When I glanced over to see her up and awake beside me in the early hours of the day, I was reminded of what an incredible friend she was to do this, all for me and some darned race.

We made our way to the transition area while it was still dark out. There were plenty of other people on foot; once again, that headlamp came in handy to keep us from running into them. There were huge industrial lights on tall poles at the transition area that illuminated everything. It was an interesting set-up: body marking at the entrance to transition, portable bathrooms far outside it, and a front and rear entrance/exit. It was definitely necessary to walk through the process involved in this race. It was different from all my other races up to that point. They didn't allow any athletic supporters inside the transition area. Crystal had to make her way around to the other side of the area with my bag so I could roll my bike through while I was getting body marked. Once I got to my spot, Crystal hoisted my bag over the fence so I could put its contents in place in my transition area and then hand the empty bag back to her. After that, it was time to warm up and empty my stomach and bladder in preparation for the race start. I still felt full and even a bit bloated. I just thought it meant I would have my strongest race thus far: I was chock-full of great food, protein, and nutrients. Boy, was I wrong.

When I am ready to race, I hate waiting around. Too much time gives my nerves a chance to start firing with doubting thoughts. I loved what Meredith Kessler said about "Getting comfortable feeling uncomfortable." It rang true for me when thoughts nagged at me while I watched others start. I asked myself, What if I couldn't do it? What if I couldn't do it at Kona? What if I disappointed others? Myself? I started wondering if I was only doing it for the attention. I wanted to know what it was all about and if I was doing this for the right reasons. I questioned if I should just do races as training. I was tired of training and I realized that my slower pace might have been a rebellion against the clock. Despite all the time and effort that I had put into training, I still felt like I was an outsider among the top athletes. And here I was, competing side by side with them in the same races. I didn't understand why I was thinking all of this since my body was just as capable as any. I realized maybe I was thinking too much. I just didn't know for sure. It could have been a bodily defense mechanism to avoid getting hurt, but I felt strong and didn't want anything to stand in the way of getting to Kona. I decided to re-wire whatever these limiting beliefs were with these new beliefs: I have done the training to finish this race well and hold my head up, and to perform in Kona. It is my destiny to compete in Kona and that's what this race is setting me up to do.

During the race, I realized I had either eaten too much, started too soon, or made my drink mix too strong. When I started to take in nutrition, I doubled over with stomach cramps that lasted until I backed off and slowed my speed. I had gels on the course for the run and tried the Hammer gels, but my system didn't like them. I brought PowerBar gels, but my new race kit had small pockets in back and I had only fit one in before leaving the transition area. From this race, I learned the lesson that I should put freezing gels in my hat. My bike watch died at the first mile and I left my backup watch at the transition point, so I ended up needing to ask people along the way how long we were into the race. I realized I was making rookie mistakes. And, by beating myself up over them, it was only draining my energy further. Better to learn from the mistakes, making mental notes on what to do differently next time. Making rookie mistakes is to be expected. It was my reaction to them and what I did with them that made the difference.

My transitions should have been two minutes or less, and they were still too slow. You have to remove your goggles and swim cap and climb out of the wet suit, put on your socks, biking shoes, helmet, sunglasses, race number, cooling sleeves and sunscreen, and run with your bike to the end of transition—which in this case was the size of a football field. Because the wet suit is wet, it alone can take two minutes to remove! Afterwards, when I saw the videos of myself running after the race, I looked exhausted and wasn't taking my normal strides.

I realized I needed to practice my transitions more, but some of the problems came from making errors. I ended up going out the bike entrance and had to go back through and around. I burned through five minutes making mistakes.

Cambridge brought me face to face with a problem I had encountered before. I was bored during the middle miles of the biking and running courses. The race time didn't matter much to me by the time I was running. I was tired of training. The one thing bringing me a sense of vitality was talking to people, hearing their stories, or complimenting them. I relied a lot on the other athletes and the crowd to catch a new sense of energy and adrenaline—the rush of the cheering crowd was like a drug. What I later realized is I had come face to face with internal versus external motivation. I had been using external motivation to complete the training for this race and it felt empty. When I switched to internal motivation, finding something in it that sparked excitement and meaning for me, it brought the adrenaline and powerful fuel to propel me to a strong finish. Big lesson learned!

I was surprised that my swim felt good since I swam off course. It was the first time I had stayed with my wave during a race and I knew I could have pushed myself a bit harder. As I ran, my right knee and hamstring started hurting. My lower back and my left foot were bothering me. The last four miles of the race, my quads started hurting.

Subconsciously, I was afraid of being slow or sub-par. I realized after Cambridge that I was lacking consistency. Even though I ran well on the track, it didn't seem to translate to the race. Total race time: 6:16:10, swim; 44:00, bike; 3:01:09, run; 2:22:00. The race didn't seem like a step toward Kona. But looking back, it was a step I had to take. I was now armed with the knowledge of what I could focus on that would produce the best results in Kona.

Chapter 11

Half Ironman

I was already signed up for the Half Ironman Triathlon Series (HITS) July race; otherwise I would have cancelled it. Gretchen said I could either choose a half Ironman, or do the distances myself. I thought the additional race experience and course challenge would be helpful. But by the time July rolled around, I was tired and still had a long road ahead of me while I trained to reach Kona.

Early in the summer, a forest fire near the HITS location, Fort Collins, Colorado, had deposited soot and ash in the reservoir where the swim had been planned. Rather than risk the health of the athletes, the HITS director decided to change the venue to Sterling, a small farming community in northeast Colorado. There was little to no shade in Sterling, and it could be hot and windy. This would be more Kona-like. Still, I wasn't excited about the new location.

Glenn, my dear friend of 20-plus years, had family in Fort Collins and was going to visit to coincide with my race and to cheer me on. I was excited about that because I always like to have people I know watch me race. It challenges me to do my best and show them what I can do. With Glenn, I was particularly excited because he had never seen a triathlon before, and I guess I wanted to impress him with my athletic ability. We had been talking, and he was interested in the prospect of seeing a triathlon, an Ironman to boot. Also, Ruby had already agreed to come with me. Fort Collins would have been a day-trip and she would have been able to return home after the race. Sterling is further away, and we'd have to go up early, get a hotel room, and stay overnight. Glenn could not take the entire day plus travel time to come see the race when the venue was moved, so he was not coming.

I decided to "man up" and deal with it like any professional with my experience would. After all, I was going to Kona with the top triathletes in the world, right? I secured a cheap hotel for Ruby and myself, and we worked out our plan. I had found some of the cooling sleeves I would need in Hawaii, and was looking to try them out. They were a new thing for me, and at least that generated a bit of excitement.

Once we made the long drive to the venue, we dropped our stuff off at the hotel and headed out so I could finish a quick training ride. Since it was a scorcher, Ruby asked if I wanted to try the cooling sleeves. They are made of a thin, white, silky-type material that wicks away sweat to the outside of the sleeve so it can evaporate and keep you cool. They are white so they don't absorb the heat of the sun, and they fit snugly on each arm between your wrist and deltoid shoulder muscle. I put them on with my riding jersey. She stayed with the car and gear until I returned. Immediately, they felt like arm warmers, not coolers. They seemed too thick, and even though they were white, they didn't seem to reflect the heat and sun. They seemed to absorb it. I had asked the guy in the store if they needed to be wet to work and he said no, so I wondered if they were working properly. Gretchen said they should make me feel a bit cooler with or without being wet. I definitely was not feeling cooler!

I ran through the gears: Chrissie, my tri bike, was in perfect running shape. My mechanic had tuned her up after we returned from Cambridge, and she looked and felt brand new. I switched into harder gears, went into "aero" position, and started cruising the roads, feeling the surfaces and thinking about the race. I was getting in my training ride and knew I would deal with whatever the course had to dish out. Because it was being held in a place that wasn't pretty, had a real rural vibe that I didn't connect with, and there was nothing in Sterling I cared about, I didn't even bother to drive the course. In Ft. Collins, where the race was originally planned, the town is pretty, and the Colorado State University campus gives it an energetic vibe. I find that if a race location has interesting topography to look at, it holds my interest more.

Having put the so-called cooling sleeves in my jersey, I was sweating profusely when I got back to the car. Ruby asked how the sleeves worked, and I told her they didn't. She asked if I was going to wear them on race day. I said I was going to return them to the store and find others that actually worked! I put my bike away and off we went to check out the reservoir and go for a swim. My sister does not love swimming, even though she knows what great exercise it is and would love to be good at it. She also couldn't stand up to the heat like I could, and it was burning our feet. So, she gladly jumped in with me! The reservoir was shallow and I could walk pretty far out. There were a few other swimmers and a couple triathletes, but not many people overall. The water looked like dirt, which I tried not to think about. I just concentrated on how cool the water was on my hot skin.

The buoys were in place for the race, so I swam to the first one and enjoyed stretching my arms and shoulders and kicking my legs a bit. I turned at the first buoy and made my way to the finish portion of the beach in a straight line. It was hard to see anything with the water being so brown. I had to lift my head up on each full stroke to sight the target. The swim finish markers weren't in place yet, so I had to imagine where they would be and make my way there. Ruby had floated around a bit and waded over to the same spot. When I emerged, we discussed how the swim course would probably be laid out.

Once out of the water, we both put on dry clothes and made our way up to the transition area to have a look around. The race coordinators were not letting anyone park close to the transition area—people had to park about a half-mile away and walk down for the pre-race meeting. It was still scorching hot, and the walk was on sand with stickers. I was growing annoyed. As we walked down the sticker-infested, sandy path, an athlete going the opposite direction mentioned that I should wear good running shoes for sand. I stopped dead in my tracks to ask him more about the run course surface condition. He said he had done a training run on some of it and it was pure sand. This can make for tough running, especially with brutal temperatures on treeless ground. I questioned him and he suggested

I ask the race director at the pre-race meeting. I said I would do just that and thanked him for mentioning it.

At the pre-race meeting, it became clear that this was the first race the HITS organization had done in the area. Based in upstate New York, HITS, Inc. is a special events management company primarily focused on producing endurance sports events and hunter/jumper horseshows. I could tell the otherwise-experienced director was sugarcoating things a bit. The company was used to putting on equestrian events. At that point, I remembered hearing some athlete acquaintances say they no longer signed up for HITS races because triathlons weren't their specialty.

I asked the director point blank about sand, and he said vehemently there was only a bit of sand at the beginning of the course. I realized that even if the whole course was sandy, there was really nothing anyone could do about it. I had no other running shoes with me, and I certainly wasn't going to buy a new pair (in Sterling, no less!). Unless I was prepared not to race, I'd better just do the best I could. Needless to say, the small amount of excitement I'd had was gone. My heart went out to the race director. He seemed like a naturally nice, giving man and was giving every possible effort to make us feel good about the race and venue.

After picking up the race packet and information on how this race and transition would be different, I wondered if I was risking injury by taking part. Maybe I was just being overly worried and a bit superstitious, not wanting anything to stop me from Kona. I shook the thought off, thinking I was in great shape and still needed the build of this race for my total volume. I thought of it like steps leading to a pinnacle. Back at the hotel, Ruby and I settled in, after putting my stickers and race numbers on everything. There wasn't anything at all to do in Sterling, even on a Saturday night. We had brought our own food for dinner and knew we needed to get to bed early for the next day. We watched a bit of television, confirmed wake up and departure times for the next morning, and went to bed. I didn't sleep well that night—I kept waking up and looking at the clock, worried I would oversleep. I think this was happening because I just wanted to get up, get this race over with, and have it behind me. I think I was tired of racing. I didn't care about this race. My heart just wasn't in it. As anyone who has experienced doing something they feel they have to do versus something they want to do knows, there is no excitement or energy. There is only forcing yourself to do it and hoping it will pass quickly.

The next morning came fast and it promised to be another scorcher. By the time we loaded my stuff into the transition area, it was already hot. At least Ruby would have a pavilion to wait under during the race, unlike most previous events she'd been to. After I saw everyone's stuff lined up in transition, I realized it was a pretty small race. There were perhaps seven rows in transition, compared to the 10 to 15 I'd seen in others, and the rows were shorter. When we all lined up on the beach for a mass swim, I noticed how small the group was and realized how unpopular both the race and venue were. I wondered how many athletes had dropped out when the race was moved. Well, live and learn, I thought. With that, the gun sounded and we were off. Since there was only one mass wave, I lined up near the back and waited for everyone else to take off, figuring that the swim time didn't matter much for this race.

The water felt good and the swim went well, until I came around the last buoy and was heading back toward the shore. There was a white boat off to the right where we needed to line up. We needed to run up several flights of concrete stairs and across the pavilion to the transition area, and there was not much on the beach to see from the water. I ended up sighting off the boat since it was easier to see, and I got off course, which cost me some time. The swim seemed to take forever, and when I jumped out of the water and ran up, I realized it had taken forever. My bike was the only one left in the entire transition area—again. I felt so slow!

Right then, it would have been easy for me to give up and not finish the race. I didn't care about it at all. It wasn't required to get me to Kona, it had been nothing but a big pain so far, and it wasn't going well. I remembered talking to my friend, a former pro Ironman, who told me that professional athletes often don't finish races for those very reasons. I remembered telling him it didn't make sense to me. He said they had to answer to sponsors and if they weren't going to have a great race, the sponsors didn't want their bad results to be out there for all to see. I could understand that decision for sponsored athletes, but I was not one of them.

Instead, I reflected on my own strength of character and asked myself why I would quit something I had committed to do, not to mention had paid money for and allocated time to this race. Although I didn't like the location and many other features of this race, I resolved to finish. I felt that if I didn't finish this race, I would be saying to myself it's okay to quit when things aren't going my way. I didn't want to get into that mindset. I thought about Julie Moss, who in the1982 Ironman lost control over her legs in the final few feet of the World Championships and pulled herself across the finish line. Julie Moss had stayed in my mind for 30 years. If anyone could have quit, she could've; but she didn't. She said that she would finish no matter what. Even though the race was trivial, not the world-championship, I felt the same way. I had considered this race trivial because it wasn't a WTC sanctioned half Ironman. It was just the Half Ironman distance. There was no magic, no large field of athletes, and no caché to it like at a sanctioned Ironman race. This is where my thinking was flawed. I wasn't connecting the dots that doing well in this race and pushing through my barriers would help me do well in Kona. I saw them as two separate things.

Out on the bike, I thought about this even more and realized my life had been that way. Once I decided to do something, I was going to do it. No matter what it took, no matter what it was. Otherwise, why even bother to decide to do it? In that moment and with that realization, I recommitted myself to the race, working through my limiting beliefs.

As I continued on the course, I again felt like I was being tempted to give up on myself. The race director had explained there were some gentle hills on the course. On one of the main stretches, all I could see ahead was what looked like a mountain pass to climb. I thought, Well, I'd better get used to expecting the unexpected. This seemed like a good lesson in this line of racing. No Ironman course was going to be easy and the training to get there wouldn't be, either. I'd recently heard the saying, "Get comfortable being uncomfortable," and I thought these two ideas sounded like good mantras.

Racing pushed me out of my comfort zone in ways I did not expect. At the beginning of the year, I had also decided on two songs that described my actual mantra, after Gretchen asked me what they would be. The songs were Switchfoot's "This Is Your Life" and Rob Zombie's "Never Gonna Stop Me." Here's why. "This Is Your Life" was relevant because one of the lyrics is, "This is your life, are you who you wanna be? This is your life, is it everything you dreamed that it would be?" This always struck me at my core because I wanted to be and achieve more, and it added the perspective that this is your life—MY life—not someone else's. That made me feel a sense of urgency. "Never Gonna Stop Me" was relevant because it was a strong mantra to all of the naysayers that they can never stop me. No matter what, I will find my way. It was also a confirmation of my own strength to not let anyone stand in my way. All these ideas kept swirling in my head, and pretty soon I could hear the songs in my mind and sang them to myself throughout the bike course, which was a formidable opponent.

Once I finished the bike leg and got into transition, Ruby stood at the fencing and told me everyone was having trouble with the sand or heat or both. She said plenty of athletes had been treated for heat stroke or limped across the finish line because of the sand. "Oh, great," I said, and thought, Well, I'm about to get even more uncomfortable than I've been all day. I tried to imagine it was Kona so that I could get through it. I thought about shortening my stride a bit to ease up on my legs, and thought it direr than any other race because I didn't have any recovery time if I got injured before Kona. I poured water and ice on my head the entire way to avoid heat stroke.

The run course was an out and back—starting at one point, running out to another point, and then going back to the original starting point. I never liked these, because all your time spent going to the turn-around point shows how long of a return trip it is. If the course is a loop, then it's easier because you are always seeing something new. On an out and back, you see familiar things and say to yourself, "Oh, I remember seeing that, I've still got a long way to go." The initial, sandy leg traversed through the North Sterling State Park where the reservoir was located. It took us out by way of a dirt and rock road to a desolate turnaround point with no trees or shade whatsoever. What a test to see what I was made of! At that point, I didn't even care about my time. I just wanted to make it through without collapsing or sustaining an injury. Another runner going the other way told me to watch out for rattlesnakes, as they were known to be in the area. It took a lot of faith in so many things for me to keep going. It took faith in my training that I knew what I was doing. It took faith in my abilities and strength that I wouldn't find a weak point in my body on the difficult terrain and injure myself. And it took faith in something so much bigger than myself to even be here and going for this goal in the first place.

Because it was so hot, all of us were moving slowly. We chatted about our misery more than at any other race I had been in. I seemed to have camaraderie with every female racer, two of whom said they had been following me, using my pace to keep going. When I heard that, I thought we all must be out of our minds, because I hadn't been keeping a consistent pace. I was just trying to run as much as I could between water stations, and I knew I would be walking some of the more sandy sections instead of burning my already spent calves trying to run them. I had poured so much water and ice on my head that my socks and shoes started sloshing. I didn't know which was worse: having soaking feet and blisters or heat stroke!

I soldiered on, and when I got to the final two miles and back into the park, I saw a steep, long uphill section, and that angered me. I was so over this stupid race that I started cursing as I made my way up, running at first and then walking. After that came the deep sand I had encountered on my way out—and I knew it would be this way every step to the finish line. My left foot and right knee started hurting and then I began to be scared that I was tempting fate. I kept thinking, Nope, I refuse to let anything bad happen (conquering a limiting belief). I began limping and toughened my resolve to finish no matter what. The end of the race is a sandy hill that goes for an eighth of a mile; I was absolutely spent by that time. I was hot, sweaty, and sandy and my eyes hurt. My right knee was really hurting, and I was running with a limp, almost shuffling. I pumped my arms to give me momentum to make it the rest of the way up the sandy hill, and then I came out on the concrete path that still continued uphill to the final 500 feet to the finish line. The announcer congratulated me as I came across the line. At that point, I didn't even care about my time. I was just glad to be done with this race and wanted to wipe this day from my memory as fast as I could.

Ruby was waiting for me at the top of the ramp at the finish line. She could tell that something was wrong. I told her I was hurting but thought I would be fine. She said she saw plenty of athletes come in limping or worse, or having to have intravenous fluids administered by the emergency crews on hand for the race. Neither of us had ever seen this before, and it was scary to think it could actually happen in any race. Because of this, it became crystal clear the line I was walking in training and racing.

We made our way to transition so I could change clothes, use the bathroom, and get something to eat. Ruby joined me and we sat down to eat after I stretched and had my recovery drink. We continued to watch athletes walk or jog through the finish. Two more athletes in the pavilion needed intravenous fluids, and they were both way younger than me! I was proud of myself for finishing and sticking to my plan for hydration and nutrition. It had always seemed to serve me well. I'd had no stomach upset at this race and was happy things were going well for me, especially compared to some of the athletes. Ruby and I couldn't wait to get out of Sterling, so we used a camping shower in the park, changed into clean, dry clothes, and Ruby drove us home.

KEY FOUR

HIRE A COACH

Chapter 12

Find the Coach Who's Right for You

Verbalizing to Crystal and Ruby my lifelong dream of Kona was the catalyst for me to change. And beyond that, I had no earthly idea of what to do or how to go about getting to Kona.

I thought I want to do something I've never done before, so perhaps I should do something different than I've done before. As I was thinking this, an acquaintance shared about a cousin who competed in Kona and who had hired a coach. It was a big key to their success. I had not thought of this before!

This set in motion my search for a coach who had the capacity to push me to achieve my goal. I interviewed three, and Gretchen seemed perfect because she had competed in Kona three times and was number three in the world at age 50. She had also trained many athletes who went to Kona.

Given the fact that I didn't have any triathlon credentials on my athletic resume, she was a little reluctant to take me on. I had to talk her into coaching me by telling her that Kona was my lifelong dream, and I was a person who excelled and prevailed over challenges. I promised I would do whatever it took to get there. The last thing I told her was that I was the sort of athlete who never gave up. When I put my mind to something, I never stop until I achieve my goal. I told her that I would prove I was consistent and committed with every minute and every hour of my training. That was how I convinced her to take me on. I told her I had an iron will and would be the most consistent athlete she had. That was the starting point of my training with my coach.

I had interviewed one other coach but didn't hire her because she had never been to Kona and none of her athletes had qualified for the Ironman in Kona. Those were the most important requirements since Kona was my goal. Ultimately, I chose Gretchen because she had the capacity and the mindset to push me as she had pushed others. I had to dig deep and ask myself: Am I willing to do everything it takes to get to the goal, bar none? I had to make changes, and I needed a coach who would push me and my buttons continually to make those changes.

My husband disagreed with me about hiring a coach. He felt that paying for a coach was only for well-off celebrities, and I didn't have the right to it as an amateur. According to him, I should follow his training schedule and ideas until I reached a level of achievement that warranted a coach. I thought the complete opposite. I didn't know how I would do something I had never done before unless I worked with someone who had experienced it. Through Keller Williams, I learned that if I wanted different results, I had to do things differently. I pointed out to him that maybe that was why he had not achieved his goals in adventure racing and ended up injured. I had no intention of following his path. I know that my response didn't sit well with him.

The truth is, I didn't really prepare emotionally or mentally for The Ironman in Kona. I had no idea how tough I would need to be. I had a dream, a goal, and I wanted to do whatever it took to get there. Goal setting has always been imperative for me, and that's where a coach came in— I knew if I wanted to get anything done, I would need to set a goal to know what I had achieved. My coach would be there to help me set goals that would stretch me, to help me see what I couldn't see, and to push me through the discomfort to do more than I thought I could to reach my goal. She would push the buttons that enabled me to expand.

Chapter 13

Kicking Up My Swimming Abilities

I realized I needed more than just one primary coach. Swimming was my weakest area, and I needed to kick up my swimming abilities, so I added a swim coach to my triathlon coach for extra emphasis in that area.

By fall, I had become fast enough to swim a 100, which is four lengths, in just above two minutes. I had accomplished this through tons of practicing. Most days I felt like I was growing gills, and my skin always smelled of chlorine. Always. I had gotten better at breathing more efficiently, and was starting to see the first signs of a smooth, powerful stroke that propelled my body forward. It would still be very slow for me to put it all together. It was suggested I join Masters, which is essentially a swim team for post-college adults. My swim coach, "Dick," had missed qualifying for the Olympics in 1996 by one second and was an All-American and NCAA Champion in butterfly, free-style, and backstroke.

He was tall and thin, with blonde hair, white teeth and overall good looks. He was mild-mannered until he became frustrated that you weren't shaping up to his expectations.

What they didn't tell me is that the Masters swim team was super-fast! For practice, I would get up as the sun rose and go to the local community college at 5:30 a.m. on Monday, Wednesday, and Friday to swim for 90 minutes. When I first arrived at the college pool, I was told that I'd swim in the last lane—the gutter lane—as the newest and likely slowest member of the group. It was an accurate placement because I saw right away that I was much slower than the other swimmers. There were about 15 swimmers when I first began with them. Though they didn't look the part, they certainly could swim. In the first speed drill, I think every single swimmer lapped me. I felt pathetic after that drill, but grew more determined to become a better swimmer.

When I started swimming in Masters, I felt unsure of myself, like a fish out of water. I needed a significant amount of help with my technique. We swam 2,000 to 2,400 yards a day—100 yards is four lengths. Each Monday, we worked on distance; Wednesdays, we focused on technique; and Fridays, on speed. I despised swimming on Fridays. I felt like my lungs were going to burst most of the time; the rest of the time, I felt like I would sink. One day during practice, Dick said, "You have a terrible feel for the water." This didn't help my self-esteem.

It was difficult getting up repeatedly at the wee hour of 3:30 a.m. to do workouts before swim and work—some days I wasn't sure my legs would hold me up. The tough emotional aspects of learning to improve when the girls were rude to me compounded the physical component. Adding to that, my own coach, Dick, said I needed to know my place around faster athletes and not act uppity.

He would stand on the pool deck and call out what our set was going to be. The sessions were 90 minutes: there would be a warm up, main set, and cool down. The warm up and cool down would be approximately 15 minutes each, leaving the main set at an hour. He would call out all at once what the entire warm up, cool down, or main set would be and would not write it down anywhere. He expected us to remember the entire set from his calling it out to us just two times. This is what a main set looked like:

- **4 x 250 alternating breathing pattern**

25 yards breathing every 6th stroke, 50 every 5th stroke bilateral breathing (breathing to both sides alternately), 75 every 4th stroke, 100 every 3rd stroke (bilateral breathing)

- **4 x 100 choice of strokes**

(choose any stroke except free-style)

- **8 (reps) x 50 yards windsprint down, slow stroke back rest:15 (15 seconds) between each length**

(swim each windsprint without taking a breath)

- **8 (reps) x 25 yards windsprints resting:30 (30 seconds) between each length**

(swim each length without taking a breath)

- **4 (reps) x 100 IM (this is done by 25 yards each stroke, butterfly, back stroke, breast-stroke and free-style) resting: 45 (45 seconds) between 100**

(if you are not tired from the wind sprints, reduce your rest time to:30)

Dick would stand on the pool deck where the fastest swimmers were, at the opposite end of the pool from me, and the pool had 15 lanes. One day we were into the main set and I lost track of what we were doing and looked at what the swimmers in the other lanes were doing so I could emulate them. Apparently, I wasn't doing what I was supposed to, and Dick yelled across the pool, "Hey, if you aren't going to do the set I assign, you can leave right now! Get out, get out of the pool," he said, walking quickly toward me. I was so surprised that I didn't know what to do, and my mouth wouldn't work. He came over to my lane and said it again, and when I still couldn't answer, he said, "What, nothing to say to that? Look, what are you going to do? Swim my program or yours?" I managed, "Yours." Luckily, my lane mate Shawn stuck up for me. Shawn was a good, strong swimmer and had swum in the Coast Guard off the eastern shore. He was training for his first triathlon after being inspired by my dream of getting to Kona. We helped each other. I was helping him get into shape and understand triathlon and he was helping me get better at swimming. Shawn said to Dick, "Hey, we forgot the rest of the set because it's so long and you don't write it down. If you write it down somewhere, we can be sure we follow it."

Dick replied, "No, I'm not going to write it down anywhere. If you are too stupid that you can't remember the entire set, then you should just leave now."

Wow. I was just flabbergasted. I didn't know what to do. I was crying in the pool, and I'm not a person who cries easily. Shawn saw me and said, "Hey, it's going to be okay. We know the set now, and let's just get to it before he gets mad again and does throw us out of here." With that, he led for the rest of the set and I simply followed. Boy, it's hard to swim when you are crying. I just kept thinking, Dick is going to throw me out of here and then where am I going to go to train for the swim at Kona? I was terrified of him. Even though he was good-looking, when he raised his voice it reminded me of when I was abused as a little girl, and I just froze and couldn't talk.

After we finished the swim practice, one of the faster swimmers, Sheila, approached me in the locker room. She came up to me and said, "Hey, I just want you to know that Dick has threatened to throw me out of practice several times. Don't let him get to you. He's just a jerk." I looked up and tears filled my eyes again. She saw how upset I was and gave me a big, long hug, saying, "It's going to be okay. Everything is going to be just fine. Just listen to what he says and do whatever you have to do to remember it. Maybe you can remember the first half and your lane buddy can remember the second half. But, don't let him get to you. You are way better than he is."

I was so grateful to her. Most of the other faster swimmers didn't talk to me much. It was like we were in two different worlds. They would be nice or cordial to me, but I could tell they didn't really relate. Sheila was an exception. She spent time with me outside of practice to teach me how to float and ride on the water tension to become more relaxed. I finally started feeling more comfortable in the water.

For reasons unknown to me, I've always held a deep-seated fear of the water, even though I went on cruises, loved the beach, and visited places like Lake Powell. When I started training, I swam begrudgingly and never felt comfortable.

While I was working on swimming, my shoulder started hurting every day and felt fatigued. I talked about the pain with my swim coach, so he videotaped me. It was a horrible experience for me to watch it. I thought I was making progress and had come far along. Watching the tape showed me how much I still needed to improve. My right arm went off to the right, which was why I always got off course. It was never as straight as it should have been and was normally bent, which was the cause of my shoulder pain. The video showed my left arm angled a little, but in the middle of the stroke, my hand would go parallel to my body, which didn't give me any propulsion. I was angry and frustrated with myself, yet I was so glad to know what I had been doing that whole time to still stink at swimming.

Dick wasn't helpful and it seemed to me he took every opportunity to single me out and point out how terrible a swimmer I was. I believe he was genuinely trying to help me, but it was tough to see at the time. Over the next few months, I swam consistently and rarely missed a practice. I even swam when I went out of town or if I was away on business. I wanted to get better and master it.

The number of swimmers doubled in January, and I had to share a lane with a couple of new people, which made it more challenging. I was pushed to swim faster. We started a test called 10 x 100s on the first Monday of each month. We would swim ten rounds of 100 yards (four lengths) as fast as we could. It was an all-out sprint. We would only take one-minute rests between, which is not enough time to recover, so by number five, you feel the lack of oxygen and are breathing really heavy and still have five more reps to go. I would feel my feet start to tingle due to oxygen deprivation and thought, One of these days, they are going to have to rescue me from the bottom of the pool. It was scary, but I forced myself to do it. We were timed for each round and had the same amount of rest in between. When we first started the 10 x 100s, I felt like I would die. By the third 100, I was ready to quit, and by the last one, I thought I would end up at the bottom of the pool and felt like puking. My times were 2:16 for each 100; the coach told me we would repeat the exercise once a month to track my progress. That wasn't something I looked forward to.

In addition to the swimming workouts, my tri coach, Gretchen, added plyometrics, also known as plyos, and functional strength training. Plyos are focused on having muscles exert force for a short time with the goal of increasing power and speed. The training conditions increase the athlete's muscular power and include resistance exercises so the muscles stretch, then shorten. Plyometric exercises like lunges, squats, core work, and hopping are often among the typical exercises for professional and amateur athletes. Plyometrics provided a nice break from weight lifting and were challenging. I even jumped rope, which I loved. The plyometric routines often rotated from low to high intensity workouts.

In all of these cases, I trusted my coaches to push me to stretch my comfort zone and to keep moving beyond where I thought my own limits were. The great thing about a coach is sometimes they can see how far you can stretch yourself when it may be hidden to you.

Chapter 14

The Lottery

On Sunday, April 15, 2012, I woke early in the morning and went through my normal routine of preparing for my long run of the week. It was six months until the Kona IM WC, and it was the day of the lottery. The list of the lucky 100 athletes winning a Kona slot was posted on that day. I tried to stay positive and believe I would get a spot in spite of the fact there were approximately 90,000 applicants and only 100 spots. All the names are pulled at random from the tens of thousands of entries for the 100 spots to the World Championships. Some athletes enter the lottery every year and don't come up with a spot. The year before, I had paid $100 for two entries to the lottery but wasn't surprised when I didn't get a spot. It hadn't hurt to try, I thought.

That Sunday morning, I prepared myself to get out and run even though I didn't feel like it. I looked outside to see a gray, gloomy sky overhead. I quickly turned my thoughts around and decided not to question myself or my motives. I told myself not to give up on Kona. I knew I just needed to get out there and keep running. It was, after all, about mental toughness and perseverance, so I thought: I should get out and do my run and check the list when I get back.

For the first part of the run, I had a really difficult head wind with snow and sleet. There was no one out there, just me. I felt alone. I asked myself why it needed to be such a tough run, but reminded myself that this was all part of my preparation for Kona. After all, Kona would be the most significant test of my body and will that I had faced.

I wondered whether or not my name was on the list for Kona. I reminded myself of everything I had learned and accomplished in the two years of training I'd just completed. I had become a triathlete and a more mature athlete. I had gained a tremendous amount of knowledge. I prayed as I ran and repeated the words, God, if it is time for me to go, I know you will put my name on the list, and if it isn't my time, I accept it. Right after this, a great feeling of peace came over me. I felt like I was floating on the way home as I uttered the prayer. I told Him that if my name wasn't on the list, I would stick to the plan and just keep going.

My sister Ruby was waiting for me so we could go visit Aunt Mary. As we were about to leave, I checked the list because if I didn't, the question would nag at me all day. I went into my home office, sat down in front of the computer and started pulling up the list. My heart was racing as I scrolled through last names, first names, states, and ages. I saw another person with the name Brown from Colorado, but kept scrolling when I realized it wasn't me. There were already two people from Colorado on the list and I figured there would not be a third, but I remained hopeful.

When I went to the next page, I saw it: Karen Brown of Littleton, Colorado. My name was on the list! I rubbed my eyes and kept looking again and again, unable to believe it was there. I knew God had His hand in putting my name on that list. I yelled for my sister and she said, "Your name is on the list, isn't it?" I jumped up and we started screaming and hugging. I thought of everything I had been through in the previous two years to prepare for Kona. I thought of all my icons who had been there, and now I had my ticket and would race where they raced! As it sank in over the next few minutes, all I could think of was what to do next. For the time being, I needed to stick to the training schedule. I could think of all the arrangements later.

I called Crystal and she answered even though she was traveling. When I told her that my name was on the list, she said she always knew I would get there. I invited Crystal and Ruby to come with me to Kona since they believed in me and supported me. I knew they had done things they never would have done if they did not love me. They weren't just fans; they were my biggest supporters, with me on every part of my journey.

It turned out that Allan's friends received lottery spots, too, but they said they would still do the qualifying race to get there "the real way" and substantiate their spots there. I knew I was doing the race in Kona to prove myself, and I thought they should be thankful that their names were on the list. I wondered if they might resent me and be upset because my name was on the list for Kona so fast. I knew I was meant to go to Kona, and this was right in line with the vision I always had of what it would feel like to be there.

Once I found out I'd received one of the lottery spots for Kona, I booked the bike transport, since it helps you get your bike there a few days before the Ironman. It filled up fast because it made transporting the bike easier. There's no need to break down the bike and use a box, or to pay the airline to transport it, then have to put it back together upon arrival. All I needed to do was unscrew the pedals and have it put on a truck. The transport would bring the bike and it would show up in the transition area. I could put my pedals on and be all ready to go.

Normally, I would have trusted everything would be okay, but I kept thinking it all through to make sure I would be prepared. Over the summer, I called the bike transport company, and they said they did not have a reservation under my name and didn't have any room left. Since they insisted I didn't have a reservation, I went through my e-mails to find the reservation confirmation. Once I did, they fixed the situation. I still called back every month after that to make sure they had it. I wouldn't let anything get in the way of my making it to Kona!

Chapter 15

A New Coach, A New Outlook

It was two months before Kona. I had given a presentation at a real estate conference in Keystone, Colorado the year before (2011) where I'd mentioned I was pursuing my dream of going to Kona. A man named Brandon Del Campo, a licensed real estate agent with Keller Williams, was in the audience, and he asked some challenging questions. After the session, Brandon introduced himself as a former Ironman pro. I was supposed to go to another session but became engrossed in our conversation and ended up missing it. We talked about Ironman for a few hours, and he shared his experiences with me.

At the time, I felt like God was placing people in my life who not only brought me inspiration, but who gave me the courage I needed when training and races were difficult. Brandon and I became fast friends and he offered his help and input, but he never asked if he could coach me. I think that since he had been through Ironman already, he knew how important the relationship was between coach and athlete. He was respectful of my coach Gretchen, and he often asked me questions about real estate, while I asked him questions about Ironman and different races.

When I shared the news with Brandon about getting a lottery spot for Kona, he was thrilled for me and asked if my coach would go with me. At first, I thought she would, but I found out later that she wouldn't be going because it would be too hard for her to be there without participating as an athlete. This was a major blow for me, as I had assumed she would be there as a support. Even though I knew Ruby and Crystal would go with me out of love and support, I expected my coach to be there. After all, Kona was what I had been training for over the past couple of years. The weeks following this discovery were rough on me. I was terrified at the prospect of braving Kona with no coach to give me last-minute tips or advice. I knew I was doing the training and believed God would still get me there, yet I was becoming increasingly concerned with the pain in my right leg and I wasn't getting the feedback or support I needed from Gretchen to help me heal before Kona.

Gretchen always met with me two weeks before a race to go over strategy and logistics, and she said Kona would be no exception. I agreed to meet, but I had lots of logical questions about the race: where my friends could stand to watch the race, where we should stay, and others that I hoped she could answer since she had been there three times. When I asked, she said we would discuss all of that in our pre-race meeting. I didn't want to wait that long in case bikes, cars, or scooters needed to be reserved in Kona for race day. Crystal had already checked with a couple of rental places that said they were getting down to their last rentals. We needed to get things booked. Since Gretchen had been to Kona as a racer and not a spectator, perhaps her husband Tom would be helpful. I left him a voice message, but he just sent it to Gretchen, who then sent me an email stating that, as she previously said, we would talk about it in our pre-race meeting.

While I accepted this response, I was growing more and more impatient and wondered Why is it so hard for her to just answer these simple questions so that we can get everything set up? Then, one Saturday I had a 60-mile bike ride in eastern Denver, so I had a lot of time to reflect on this and other things that had happened during the course of our relationship that just didn't sit well with me. With this and fatigue from being toward the end of very high level, intense training—which brings out emotions in me and lots of other athletes (which Gretchen actually told me to warn my family about, so they could deal with it)—I became angry. After my ride, I left her a voice mail saying I needed answers to these very simple questions, and if she couldn't answer them, maybe I should consider getting a coach who could. Short and simple message and, boy, I never could have guessed what the result would be. Since I had ridden in eastern Denver, I had varying cellular reception and 35 minutes' travel time back to my house. By the time I got home, I had an email from My Training Log saying Gretchen was no longer my coach and my training log was going to be deleted in 30 days. Along with that was a voice message from her yelling obscenities and screaming, "How dare you talk to me like that, and don't ever talk to me again! I never want to hear your name again, EVER!" She was literally yelling at the top of her lungs on the voice message. It was terrifying. I couldn't believe my ears. I had asked for a simple thing, and she blew up and fired me—all right before Kona.

I ended up talking with my sister about what had happened. I think I knew what I needed, but it helped to verbalize and discuss it with someone who had seen me through everything. I realized that although Gretchen had led me up to that point—and I had learned a lot from her about nutrition and how to train—it was time for a change, even with Kona not far off.

So in late August 2012, I asked Brandon to coach me the rest of the way. He didn't hesitate in his answer. He agreed, and answered all of the pressing questions I had. He put to rest all of my concerns about Kona and the logistics of being there. We went over some of the finer details, like figuring out places Ruby and Crystal could stand to watch and transportation options once we arrived in Kona. It helped me that he knew the layout and the local area and could give me information on problems that might arise.

I think Brandon noticed a certain level of fear I had not expressed before, because he asked what I was afraid of. I told him I was worried about being injured or in so much pain that I couldn't race or make the cutoff times—especially since Gretchen was always worried about me making them. When I told Brandon all of my times, he said there was nothing to worry about, that I wouldn't have a problem at Kona. Hearing his encouragement after he knew my times gave me the boost of confidence I desperately needed at that point. He also said that if any one of his athletes were going to Kona he would be there, too—even if it was only one person. I was grateful for his support. Knowing he would be there made me feel less uneasy.

I had been training really hard and, before the switch in coaches, had developed some pain in a couple of places that had me worried. When I switched, I immediately told Brandon about it. He was concerned and offered suggestions on how to alleviate the pain. He gave me exercises to strengthen my gluteal muscles and lower back. He also gave me the name of a physical therapist, Bob Cranny, who treats professional athletes from the Ironman, was an Ironman himself, and who still raced.

When I first went to see Bob, I tried to squelch my worry by not showing it outwardly and not giving it any credence inwardly. Bob came out to the waiting area to get me and extended his hand to make my acquaintance. He was about six-foot-three, very slender, bald except for a ring of dark hair around his head, and had dark eyes with lots of light and a great big, white, toothy smile. He had great confidence, but not arrogance. He walked swiftly and with grace. He was nicely dressed in a button-down shirt and pleated trousers with dark loafers. He asked what he could do for me, and I explained that Brandon had sent me. He immediately acknowledged Brandon and asked what Brandon was training me for. I explained that I was on my way to Kona and was worried I was on the brink of injury. He had me lay on the physical therapy table in a variety of positions to examine my hamstring and to see what my strength level and flexibility were. The whole time, he was chatting with me and asking questions about my story. After assessing what was wrong with me, he said I had nothing to worry about. He gave me some exercises and said he would see me every week until I left for the race. I readily agreed and asked if he had been to Kona. His answer was yes, he had been there three times and had one of the original Ironman trophies—a metal stick figure with a nut for the head, symbolizing that Ironmans had a hole in their heads! I had only seen a picture of the original trophy and was immediately excited to hear all about his experiences. He had to get to his next patient, so he said we would talk about it when I came back the following week.

I held him to it. I was very excited that he could fix my physical issue and could share his personal experiences of Kona so I could get a feel for what it was like.

I am certain these two suggestions—seeing Bob and following the exercises Brandon gave me—saved me from a severe injury. I had to do what I was told to do, and do it several times a day, every day. I found immediate relief through the therapy and exercises. Bob explained that I had built up adhesions over time in my upper right hamstring. Adhesions normally occur after surgery and are part of the body's natural healing process, but in my case it came after injury. Adhesions can prevent muscles from moving freely, which explained all of my pain and stiffness.

Bob warmed up my hamstring, stretched it, and then pressed on the areas with the adhesions to work them out. This stretching started out as a light practice but ended with such intensity that I winced and dug my fingers into the table. He had me do a series of leg raises that isolated and strengthened my gluteal muscles. I could also tell I was regaining strength in my hamstring, and the pain was dissipating. His methods had worked.

Brandon had me do a different series of lower and mid-leg strengthening exercises. Between all of the therapy and exercises, I was ready to run again despite the short period of time in which we had worked. My mindset kept me strong because I was determined that if I followed the protocols, it would keep me from being injured before or during Kona.

In my preparation for Kona, I learned that having a coach is essential. A coach guides you, instructs you and keeps you on track. You are bound to make zigzags in growth instead of a straight line, and a coach minimizes those and time lost with each. This is known as mastery, which typically takes 10,000 hours to obtain. Without a coach, it can take even longer.

I had a coach for swimming (to add focus and improvement in an area of weakness) and a coach for the Ironman triathlon training overall. I also learned that you can outgrow a coach, and some coaches are better for you at certain stages than others. As your level of development changes and you grow, a different coach may be the right answer. I also learned the hard lesson that when the coaching relationship is no longer working for both of you, it is time to move on and find the person who can help you do what it takes to fulfill your dream.

DO WHAT IT TAKES / SCHEDULE = GOALS

Chapter 16

Dietary Answers

When I was 14 years old, I had an eating disorder. I was playing softball, I tended to be a perfectionist by nature, and I sought control over food. Many people at the time, friends and family alike, had terse conversations with me about anorexia. I think it was a cry for attention. Now, when I see myself trying to control everything, I remind myself to relinquish that control to God. What I have come to understand is I never owned that control in the first place; I was employing the illusion of control to try to bring some semblance of order into my life.

After recovering from my eating disorder and before I started training for the Ironman, I had a good relationship with food and enjoyed vegetables and fresh fruit. I leaned toward healthy, fresh foods—but that didn't mean I couldn't enjoy a heavy, high caloric meal. I often fancied breads, cheese, and gourmet foods, as well as the occasional alcoholic beverage. I felt like I was treating myself when I had something decadent, like a chocolate dessert. I never really felt like I needed to clean my plate and seemed to naturally gravitate toward normal portions. I do love to bake, so it was easy to overdo it with sweets sometimes. When I decided to train for the Ironman, I knew that maintaining my nutrition wouldn't be a problem. I didn't think much about food and nutrition since I knew I could adjust as I trained. All of my thinking was geared toward fitness and whether I had what it would take to get there.

Because I've been athletic all my life, I developed the mentality that if I worked out enough, I could eat whatever I wanted. I am five feet, six inches tall with a small frame, so most weight gain was noticeable. I found I could always work out harder to lose weight, but I felt my best when I was around 120 pounds. I knew I felt and performed better in sports if my weight was healthy.

The doctor at the VO2 Max and lactic acid threshold testing lab told me I would need to eat carbohydrates at every meal. This was when everyone was pushing no or low carbs, so I questioned his thinking. He explained that the energy in my muscles is built from glucose, which is derived from sugars processed from carbohydrates. For endurance athletes, the glucose needs to be long burning, and training would change how long my muscles could go before lactic acid—the waste byproduct from burning glucose—built up and caused muscle fatigue, pain, and fiber tears.

The doctor also showed me on microscopic slides what glucose in muscle fibers looks like. In my mind, this confirmed his point of eating carbs at every meal. He explained that my body needed this fuel to do what I expected. I think this was the first time I really made the connection that food is the body's fuel. I was also excited at the prospect that when most people were snubbing carbs, I could eat the pasta, rice, cereal, oatmeal, potatoes, tortillas and other foods that others were bypassing. I could eat everything I loved! My calories throughout the day were often distributed into several smaller meals to compensate for my expenditure during training. My meals often consisted of protein, starches, fruits, and non-starchy vegetables. I also enjoyed healthy fats, like seeds, nuts and avocadoes.

Processed foods were never really a part of my diet, even though they were quicker to purchase and consume than cooking something more healthful at home. I felt better eating something healthy versus processed; yet I worked in a job that was demanding of my time, so I sometimes ate processed fast foods out of sheer need.

I began to think about what I could eat that would help me perform better. I looked back at the literature the doctor gave me when I was doing the testing. It explained that endurance athletes need healthy carbs because they produce stored energy. I needed to make sure I was getting them from the right sources. I knew from my athletic history that proteins were important during my training because they are a source of amino acids that help rebuild muscles, but I tried to stick with lower amounts of protein based on advice from the doctor. When I asked him about needing more protein than carbs, he explained this was a common fallacy and thought to be the way to increase muscle mass. For my training, I needed to be able to exercise for long periods of time—and a high protein diet would have been detrimental for me. I needed my muscles to elongate and become more efficient, and for that I needed long-lasting fuel from carbs and some protein.

One of the things many people don't know and learn the hard way is that you need to fuel up before and during workouts if it is a long regimen. It is important to maintain your energy levels to maintain your intensity. On my moderate or high-level exercise days, I needed to make sure I replenished because my calorie stores only lasted a couple of hours. I had often relied on sports gels and protein bars on long mountain bike rides, so these were not new to me. The difference in triathlon training was that I would take a gel before my workout, time additional gels during my workout or race, and not eat energy bars during the race. This was counterintuitive to me, but I came to understand the advantage of these methods as I built my training and started doing longer workouts and races.

My coach also educated me about using liquid nutrition high carb concentrations with salt and other nutrients like potassium, as well as energy gels and water at regular intervals during training and racing. At the time, I didn't understand that trying to force your stomach to process solid foods during a race causes you to become sick and depletes your system of what you try to put into it. I wondered how I could race without becoming hungry, and how I could take in enough calories to keep my energy level up. My coach explained that the liquid nutrition was to be mixed based on the time I would be racing. If the race was longer, the drink should be thicker, thus having more calories; and if it was a shorter race, it should be thinner with fewer calories.

A lot of the best nutrition plans fail because of mis-pacing the race. Starting out too fast at the beginning can shut down the stomach and make the refueling plan useless through lack of sodium and surplus stress. Many athletes fail to learn this and don't change their plan until it is just too late. I knew that on days I didn't follow a solid plan, I didn't perform as well and often became lethargic and mentally tired. Other athletes I knew also struggled to find products that agreed with their stomach, but I didn't have that problem. I went with the items my coach used and found they worked well for me.

The one place that I customized more was with the energy gels. They seemed to agree with me the best; I tried several brands and found two that were easy to use. If they happened to be provided at a race, it was easier than needing to pack everything myself. Unfortunately, this wasn't always the case since different races provided different gels based on what the sponsors provided. I never became sick during a race, thank goodness, but I saw plenty of other athletes who did. Sometimes, they had a hard time continuing or they would have to quit the race altogether. That was what scared me into sticking with what I knew worked. I did hate being ill, but more, this was my lifelong dream and I had put countless training hours and a lot of money into getting there. I didn't want anything to keep me from finishing.

I planned workouts so I could try different nutrition options and make sure I had what I would need for race day. I needed to plan my nutrition perfectly before, during, and after my races. I also needed to make sure I had the proper amount of fluids so I wouldn't become dehydrated and suffer a drop in my performance. I kept a training log to help me remember my nutrition and hydration choices and to be able to carry them over to my races.

When I began doing the half Ironman distances, I really began understanding how important the right nutrition is and how it fuels my body. To train for those, I did about fifteen hours of workouts a week. I felt like I was constantly hungry and eating all the time. I increased the frequency and the volume of food that I was eating—I was eating whatever I wanted and still losing weight. The doctor told me that my race weight would be about 119 and that I was walking a fine line between being too thin and the right weight. When my weight fell to 116, I was lean but I was weak and felt a bit more delicate, like I was risking injury. When I was closer to 130, I felt like I was carrying around too much weight.

I spoke with my coach about how I was feeling. She told me about a program she and her husband had been on that showed them incredible results. She explained they had been on the program together for three months and were leaner, faster, and stronger than they had been in their 20-plus year racing careers. She said all of their physical ailments—like foot pain, headaches, back pain and joint pain, had vanished. She recommended the book called Green for Life (Victoria Boutenko), and I immediately got it and started reading about a plant-based diet using green smoothies.

Green smoothies come out of the raw food philosophy, which is based on how chimpanzees eat. Their DNA is closest to that of humans and they are some of the healthiest creatures on the planet. The food they eat in the wild consists of a plant-based diet. The author of the book was a researcher and adopted the raw-food diet to help herself and her family during ongoing medical problems. When other ailments developed, she looked for something else and found green smoothies. She used three parts fruit to water, and greens like kale or spinach. The drink is packed with nutrients and the greens form perfect amino acid chains. The book answered all of my questions about getting enough protein and it made sense. Since my coach attested to its validity, I decided to give it a try.

I knew it would be important to have a good blender to mix all the fruits, greens, maccha powder (finely milled green tea), açaí juice, and other suggested items. I wore out my blender and started looking for a new one since I needed something more powerful. The best one was supposed to be a Vitamix, but the challenge was that they were around $450. Even though it had a seven-year, no-questions-asked guarantee, I still needed to come up with the money to buy it! I justified the purchase by finding a reconditioned Vitamix for one hundred dollars less, with the same warranty. I was happy that I made the purchase. It was so much faster and easier to blend the smoothies and it made them easier to drink. The recommended daily amount was a 32-ounce smoothie for breakfast, one for lunch, and a big salad with chicken, salmon, or tofu for dinner. I had already been eating salads for lunch with hardy items like potatoes, avocadoes, or tempeh, so this was not going to be much of a stretch. After one or two workouts in the morning, I was famished and could ingest the drink quickly. It was easy to blend everything and grab it and go to meetings or classes for work. It also meant I always had food with me, which had become a must when I found myself famished at the drop of a hat or feeling like I was fading out during a conversation.

What happened when I started drinking green smoothies on a consistent basis was truly eye opening. I experienced increased focus, clarity, and mental energy. After about two weeks, I lost my taste for chicken. I tried to eat it twice and thought it tasted terrible, so I stopped eating it and soon the very thought of it turned me off. After that, the same thing happened with beef and steak. My body started craving green smoothies. I finally realized what pure fuel meant for my body. My digestive tract worked a lot better and I felt healthy and lean. I also noticed less fat on my body.

The doctor who tested me as I got closer to the full Ironman distance race told me that when I got closer, I would see a drop in body fat. My coach became concerned that I was too lean and too skinny. At that point, I was training in swimming, cycling, and running and going to physical therapy, massage, the chiropractor, and yoga—which left no time to do strength training. I sometimes felt weak, but at the same time I was carrying around less mass, which made longer workouts easier. I liked rich foods and desserts; when I was drinking green smoothies, however, I did not have cravings for them. When I thought a treat sounded good and I would try to eat one, it wouldn't taste good. And I felt gross afterward. My body wanted pure fuel. I was consuming about 3,000 to 5,000 calories a day, but I wasn't really keeping track. I knew my body would keep track of it.

My pre-race meals began with some basic carb loading: pasta with a red sauce or fish, a smoothie, and bread. On the morning of a race, I would have bread, a smoothie, a carb drink, and a bit of Rockstar energy drink. My stomach never tolerated coffee well before a race, though I love my coffee in the morning. About 30-40 minutes before a race started, I would have GU Rocktane Endurance Gel. During the race, I alternated between water and Infinit—a maltodexterin carbohydrate drink, mixed with water according to the distance and time of my race. I made sure I had a plastic flask of Power Bar gels mixed with some water so I could just take a shot every hour. I alternated between these every 20 minutes. If the race was going to be hot, I added a salt solution to the Infinit to avoid muscle cramping, which is usually from a lack of salt, potassium, or both. I knew many athletes had this deficiency during a race, but luckily, I never did. For the full-length Ironman races, I ended up adding chewable glucose tables to my run belt and had one every hour to wake me up. I had a winning combination.

After races, I always tried to get some carbs into my system, replenish fluids, and replenish my sodium levels. After some of the shorter races, I would be hungry right away and eat whatever I wanted, even if it was ice cream. However, I would always have a recovery drink. Along the way, my friend shared with me ultra-athlete Rich Roll's cookbook, The Plantpower Way, which consisted of all plant-based foods and some more smoothie recipes. He broke down his recipe book into pre- and post-workout recipes. I made almost every recipe in his cookbook, and a handful of them became my new favorites. I made an art form out of eating veggie burgers and began a quest to find the best ones. The cookbook and the book, Finding Ultra, turned Roll into an inspiration for me.

Following full length races, I found that my stomach shrank and I could only consume recovery drinks in small stages, and could only get a few gulps of a smoothie down before I felt full. It was a strange feeling, needing to stretch my stomach out because it felt terrible, like it was trembling.

I learned that the body is truly a magnificent system, especially if we treat it well and give it what it needs to thrive. Doing what it takes in terms of my nutrition and understanding what it needed was an important part of my journey. I believe that the most significant part of this process was learning how to properly fuel my body and listen to what it needed. I figured out which meals worked for me and which didn't because I saw how what I ate could affect my performance and, thus, my ability to achieve my dream.

Chapter 17

Training 101

In September 2010, my coach started putting my daily training sessions on workoutlog.com, an online training program. I gave her my schedule for work, travel, family plans and other commitments, and she built training into every day and week. I created a six-part folder and put all of my test results, workout schedules, workout logs, and resources together.

Each of my short-term goals acted as a stepping stone to get to the big one. There was timing of the races and training periods. We would spend weeks at a base level, then have a build week, a peak, and then a recovery period before starting with the base level again. I started off slow, around eight to ten hours of training per week, and I trained in all three disciplines each week. The theory is that if you train hard in only one discipline, the other two will slip. This meant I would have two to three swims, bike rides, and runs each week, along with weight training and yoga to maintain flexibility. You have to take a day off to let your muscles rest, so I needed to factor that into my training regimen.

The workout regimen I was in before I decided to train for the Ironman included five days a week of cardio and weights, one to two nights of competitive sand volleyball, and some mountain biking in the summer. When I started training, I quit volleyball after playing for ten years. I felt I had done all I could there. Soon after that, I quit mountain biking since it was working different muscle groups than a road bike. My cardio training changed from either running or the elliptical machine to swimming, biking, and running. Each of my workouts helped me build my speed and endurance, rather than simply burning calories to stay in shape. Prior to training for Ironman, I was accustomed to one workout a day. When I started my official training, it was normal for me to have two workouts per day, sometimes three.

My training schedule often looked like this:

Monday: Rest day or yoga only
Tuesday: Swim in the morning, bike in the afternoon/evening
Wednesday: Weights in the morning, run in the afternoon/evening
Thursday: Swim in the morning, bike in the afternoon/evening
Friday: Swim in the morning, run in the afternoon/evening
Saturday: Long bike ride
Sunday: Long run

Sample Training Plan

WEEK Starting: **September 17, 2012**

Week Type: peak.

Coach Comments: < none >

Athlete Comments: < none >

Date	PLANNED Workout	Description
Sep 17 Mon	BikeTrainer	1 Hr Cadence Focus-
	01:00:00	Goal to teach your body to get use to a higher than normal cadence

WU: 10 min easy spin build
then 4 X 30 sec. ILT -
1 min EZ spin
4 X 30 sec spin ups

MS: 10 min- choose a gear zone2 to low 3- goal is high cadence RPM >100

3 X 3 min Hills out of saddle climbs with 2 min EZ between- Cadence on hill 70-75- no big gears today.

10 min High Cadence done
4 min @100 RPM/ 3 min @ 105 RPM/ 2min @ 110 RPM/1 min > 115 RPM

CD Remainder Easy spin

Sep 18 Tue   Swim
3800.0 yd
01:30:00

3800-600's 400's IM training- if short on time cut 4 X 75 to 2 x 75

WU 200S/ 200 K/ 200 s (600)

MS: 4 X 125 X 3 sets
round 1= swim Moderate
round 2= 75 K/50 S
round 3 = Pull (500)

rest 1 min
4 X 75 50 Swim /25 Drill (work on catchup , fingertip , hesitation- stick if you have one)

1 X 600 at 85% effort

4 x 75 as above

1 X 400 @90 % effort
4 X 75 as above
1 x 600 @ 95 % effort- record time (2500)
CD; 200 EZ swim/ Kick

   Run
01:30:00

TRACK

WU 1 min drills

MS: 1 mile repeats x 8 Rest is only 3 min EZ walk jog- get

water between

CD: 1/2 mile EZ
OOT 18-20 do what you can

Travel

Sep 19 Wed Rest

Travel

OOT 18-20 do what you can

Sep 20 Thu Run

01:05:00

TEMPO

WU: 5 min

MS: 20 min Zone 3 2 min EZ X2
15 min Zone 3 2 Min EZ

CD: 5 min

Travel

OOT 18-20 do what you can

Sep 21 Fri Brick

02:30:00

W/U: 30 minutes of 85-95 rpm small ring for 10-15 min-
add some pickups to get HR elevated

M/S: 45 minutes Zone 3- low 4- this is a focused effort-
(long....)
C/D 30 minutes 85-95 rpm small ring spinning zone 2-
low 3
Transition run 30- 45 minutes at slighty faster than
Ironman race pace
Remember I would rather you run well for 30 min then
struggle with 45. don't practice bad habbits.

Swim
4000.0 yd
01:40:00

4,000 power- 200's/100's
WU: 500 yd swim/ kick/ drill- your choice

MS:
DRILLS:
3 x 50 CATCH-UP DRILL
3 x 50 KICK- ON-SIDE W/ Fins
100 Yd swim
(400)
Power:
6 x 200 swim- 1-4 PULL 5-6 focus on high elbow and
catch(1200)

Sprint:
9 X 100 as: (15' rest) repeat x 2 rounds
Rounds done as
#1 - 50 sprint - 50 race pace

#2- 25 Race pace, 50 sprint, 25 race sprint (1800)

CD: 100 yds ez swim/ kick- pull OK

Sep 22 Sat Brick

05:30:00

Bike =5 HRs Run =30-45 min should include climb such as
deer creek, high grade or Lookout around mile 50 or so
work this ride a bit harder mileage coming down

Sep 23 Sun Run
12.0 mi
02:00:00

Run/walk Zone 2 effort

Swim

01:15:00

Attend masters class

Type	Distance	Duration
BikeTrainer		01:00
Brick		08:00
Rest		
Run		04:35
Swim	7800.0 yd	04:25
Travel		
Total Duration:		**18:00**

At the beginning, the hardest thing was planning my workouts around a new job that demanded a lot of my time and energy. When I first started the job at Keller Williams, it was not uncommon for me to work until 8 or 9 at night. I often needed to do two workouts back-to-back the following morning before going into the office. I would go to bed at 10:30 after a late dinner. I also needed to determine what workout clothing, equipment, food, supplements, and other items I would need for the next day. I packed it all up and planned where I would shower. I needed to make sure I had professional clothes and toiletries, too. It began to feel like I was living out of my car, which was full of equipment and workout bags for each discipline.

When I had two workouts in the morning, I would wake around 3:30 or 4:00 a.m. to get to the gym and swim for an hour, then run or bike for another hour. I needed to get to work by 8:30 each morning. I had to start getting massages, and went to the chiropractor to keep my bones in alignment. It helped my muscles recover so I could avoid injury from overuse. I had to fit these appointments into my weekly schedule along with everything else, so my already busy schedule became jam-packed.

My body wasn't efficient at biking or swimming yet, so I needed to work extra hard in those disciplines. I remember running at the gym before swimming, and worrying that I would drown. When I began training, I started swimming three times per week. One time, when I was swimming in the gym pool, an older gentleman came over to me from his soak in the hot tub to ask me if I was okay. I told him I was and that I was training for an Ironman. He said what I was doing didn't look like swimming! And he was making sure I wasn't drowning— yet another reminder that I needed to work on my stroke! So I started to work hard on swimming. I met with my coach, Gretchen, and her husband, who had also been to Kona. Their decision to take me on was a miracle in itself. When I first met them at the pool, I was surprised that she still agreed to work with me after seeing how awful my swim stroke was.

All my muscles hurt—especially my shoulders—when I first started training, and it was because of swimming. I learned that my shoulders shouldn't hurt, because when you swim you are supposed to use your lats and core muscles. Until I learned the proper techniques for each discipline, it felt like I was making three times the effort during each workout, all the while dealing with sleep deprivation and a high learning curve at work.

I needed to get a road bike for my training, too. There was some debate as to whether I should get a triathlon-specific bike, where the rider leans over on the flat handlebars in a bullet position, or a regular road bike which I could gear for hill climbing and meet the challenge of the course.

Hills were often my favorite part of mountain biking. I never enjoyed the downhill part of biking. I wanted to do as many tough hills as possible because I liked the challenge. My coach recommended a tri bike for efficiency since I could change the gears if I was in a hilly race.

Before I purchased a bike, my coach recommended I get fitted to see what kind of bike to buy. Some athletes end up with injuries from bikes that don't fit them. She recommended a bike fitter who fitted pros like Craig Alexander and Chrissie Wellington. His name was Todd Carver, from the company Retul.

The bike fitting was another fascinating process. I was able to get the inside scoop on what my role models were like—since Todd had fitted all of them. I went to his downtown Denver studio, and he put me on a bike/trainer, and put electrodes on my knee, hip, ankle, and shoulder. The electrodes sent information back to a computer to determine my maximum efficiency and the measurements and geometry needed to achieve it. He told me what bike brands would be best and he recommended Guru, Felt, or Cannondale—which was the same brand my coach rode. He gave me the measurements so that a bike shop or I could reassemble my bike after transporting it to a race.

I set out to find a bike. As it turned out, my coach had a bike that she was going to use for Kona the previous year, but the carbon fiber Guru—from a top of the line Canadian company—had a recall on cable glue just weeks before she was scheduled to compete. She bought a replacement bike and didn't need the Guru. When I talked with Todd about the possibility of buying my coach's bike, he looked at her measurements that he had done the year before and told me it was a great fit for me. Because it was a year old and barely ridden, I got a better deal on it than if I had bought it new from a dealer. I wanted to compare it to the Cannondale that my idol Chrissie Wellington rode, but no shops had it and no one was willing to bring it in unless I bought it—and it was significantly more expensive.

During that time, my husband vehemently argued with me, telling me I shouldn't buy such an expensive and specialized bike at the start. He thought I should buy a cheap used bike or train using my mountain bike until I could be sure I was going to get to Kona. Then I could buy a newer bike. He said that was the way he did it, and I should do it that way, too. It became a heated argument whenever I disagreed with him. He told me that if I wanted to buy my coach's bike I needed to use my own money. At the time, I had ownership distributions from the real estate office I worked in, so I used them to buy the beautiful Guru Crono. The bike was red, black, and white—which made it even more perfect since those are my favorite colors. It even came complete with Ironman logo stickers on the aero bars. I was excited that it was the bike my coach had used to qualify for a slot at Kona.

Tri bikes are different because of their geometry and the position one uses to bike. The position not only makes you more aerodynamic, you use less energy making it more efficient for long distances. The rider's position helps in wind because the biker uses their gluteus muscles to prevent burning out the leg muscles. This helps preserve as much energy as possible to run the remaining marathon. I marveled at how athletes could bike 100 miles and then step off and run an entire marathon. Training on a mountain bike wouldn't work since the geometry is different: the gearing and body position are more upright than on a tri bike. The tri bike can be more awkward. The first time I rode mine outside, the bike was nimble and I was as wobbly as a newborn calf. You need to log a lot of miles on a tri bike to be comfortable in the required position. I wasn't used to it, and it took me a while to become strong and confident on it.

I enjoyed the preparation and making sure that I had everything I needed, but there was a myriad of equipment required for training and competing: swim goggles, buoy, kickboard, swim caps, home bike trainer, separate indoor trainer wheel/tire, training videos, an ergonomic water bottle, pedals and shoes from a professional fitter, watch and heart rate monitor, and many pairs of running shoes and socks because they wore out fast. There were also energy gels; nutrition drinks; recovery drinks; salt solutions and glucose for hot workouts and races;

energy bars; and my own personal favorite, Rockstar. The supplements included CoQ10, fish oil, essential fatty acids, stomach enzymes, athletic vitamin boosters, maccha powder—the list went on depending on the specific workouts for that day or period in training.

When I began my training for the triathlon, I swam 30 minutes a day for three days per week, then ran and biked three days per week. I started yoga and began building my strength. I was training between eight and ten hours a week to build a base level of condition. I couldn't let my heart rate get above a certain level because I needed to prepare my body for the volume of training and endurance required. Although it was interesting, part of the training was monotonous.

In the meantime, my coach kept encouraging me and told me I would get there if I followed the program. The goal was to build the base level of conditioning before we increased my workouts in speed, power, and technique. I had been a mountain biker for several years and I thought I knew how to ride a bike efficiently. I was wrong. I thought I was in great shape because I worked out regularly. I quickly found out how out of shape I was, even though my body fat was healthy for my age, gender, and height.

After training for Kona for a year, I went from 125 pounds with a body fat index of 18 percent to 119 pounds and an index of 15 percent. I was training about 16 hours per week and had never felt better. The support I received from friends and family helped me stay focused on my goal and provided me with strength on difficult days. I was often asked what races were coming up, how had I done in the most recent one, and how close I was to qualifying for Kona. I received so much support that it often brought me to tears. Every time I crossed the finish line, I got choked up at the thought of the people who helped me get there.

In my first year of training, I ran 133.5 hours, biked 173 hours, swam 99 hours, and completed 133.5 hours of strength training, yoga, and cross training. All told, I completed 539 hours of training. In the first few months, I trained an average of 9 hours per week, but I increased that to 11 hours per week during the latter part of the year. By year-end, I had competed in a 65-mile bike race, a 100-mile bike race, a half-marathon, an Olympic distance triathlon, and two half Ironman distance triathlons. Each time I competed, I consistently improved my race times, and I was two-thirds of the way to qualifying for Kona.

Time Off

In September 2011 (the year before Kona), my coach told me to take the month off. When she saw my reluctance, she explained that every triathlete, no matter what level, works it out in their schedule to take one month off. Since I had no late races, she suggested I take September to go enjoy other sports that I had participated or competed in previously. At first, I thought it was great not to need to do double workouts seven days a week. After about ten days, though, I started feeling terrible and struggled with lethargy. My mind slowed and I grew bored. I called my coach and she told me I could do other workouts—just not swimming, biking, or running. I ended up doing some mountain biking, the elliptical, and trail running. I was able to enjoy the month, but couldn't wait to get back to the action of training! I craved it every day and, without it, I didn't feel special anymore.

It felt like my body and brain were dying. While training at such a high level, the body becomes accustomed to the stimulation and amount of biological chemicals that are released; without them, you can feel terrible. The more I thought about it, the more I wondered how long it had taken for my body to become accustomed to the experience and when that had occurred. I was sure it must have happened over time. Therefore, I would adjust over time, but the process seemed difficult.

It's hard to imagine that rest is a part of training, but it is. To let your mind and body rest from all of the strenuous training, it is essential to take some time off. Just as with any intense activity, time off and away from that activity gives your body a chance to rejuvenate and your mind an opportunity to let everything you've learned sink in while not adding in more. And, I found that this applied to all areas of my life, not just training.

Chapter 18

Boulder Olympic-length Race

I was preparing to run the Boulder Olympic distance race in August 2012. My training issue was to learn to leave nothing in the tank—to push myself to go faster than ever before. I was out to improve my speed. I needed to understand what it felt like to push like that and go beyond where I thought my capacity ended, i.e., leave nothing in the tank. What I came to understand is that it's not the clock that drives me in racing; it's the journey to the finish and the other people in the race.

I had practiced this racecourse a couple of times, in particular a steep climb called Old Stage Road. The road is so steep that many people get off their bikes and walk them up the hill! In past training, I had ridden on another long, steep road in Boulder called Left Hand Canyon, pushing so hard I developed a bloody nose. Having completed the longer distance of Left Hand Canyon, I thought there was no way I was walking my bike up Old Stage Road! While I watched others walk their bikes up, I was able to ride up continuously with no problem both times I rode it.

The same thing happened in the race. This surprised me since everyone knew how steep the hill was, and they should have practiced. Instead, they seemed to give up, admit defeat, and walk their bikes. I think it may be that way in life: People think something is going to be too hard and therefore don't attempt it, not realizing they could have done it if they had tried.

Frankly, I don't remember much about this race because it was so short and because I was so sick of hearing my coach telling me to be faster! I was so tired of racing. I had done six races along with training, and I liked training more than racing, in general. I would rather train hard and have it come out on race day than use races as most of my training. I just made my way through the race and didn't care about it. I remember thinking, I have to go faster, faster, faster, and because it was a "have-to" instead of a "want-to," I wasn't as motivated. Sometimes, doing what it takes involves looking at where you're not doing it and getting an understanding of your underlying motivation.

After I finished, Gretchen asked me if I had thrown up after finishing. I told her I hadn't, but that I certainly felt like I was coughing up a lung because I was pushing myself so hard. She took me back to a grassy spot by the finish line and reenacted how she wanted my finish to be. She ran to the finish so fast that she propelled herself forward and fell to the ground, having given it every remaining ounce of energy. She meant that since I hadn't finished this way, I hadn't emptied my tank completely and given it everything I had. Frankly, I had not done what it takes to finish like that.

At this point, I was sick and tired of training relentlessly and hearing that my efforts weren't enough. I was sick of it because of the compound effect of high levels of training and competing in lots of races. I got through it by finding ways that I could take little mental and physical breaks like: training in the morning one day and the evening the next so it felt like I had one 24-hour cycle off. My mental breaks were watching movies as often as I could, even if it meant watching some movies over and over. This relaxing escape for my mind refreshed my mental state, especially when I watched movies that showed transformation and someone achieving something.

It was only August and Kona was in October, so I asked my coach if I could take a breather in my training. I was thinking of taking a couple of weeks off.

She said I could take a couple of days! I reminded her of an article I had read that said overtraining was worse than undertraining, but she said that wouldn't serve me well in Kona since there were cutoff times to make and everyone there would be well-trained. I relented and took a couple of days off, then got back to training—relieved that I didn't have any more races until Kona.

That night, Gretchen sent me an article on self-talk that described a coach who tracked the changes experienced by her athletes after incorporating positive self-talk—no small feat given that people naturally gravitate toward negative thinking. The article struck a chord with me because I often caught myself saying and thinking that I sucked at swimming or that I was not a fast runner. The author suggested making a list of negative phrases and then coming up with a list of positive phrases and cue words like fast, strong, and light that you can bring to mind quickly when in need. I realized this was going to make a big difference!

I knew from my training in real estate that what you think dictates your actions, and your body and mind believe what you say to yourself and others. Words become actions. Part of what it took for me to go on and compete in Kona was going to depend on what I said to myself, so I made a commitment to embrace positive self-talk.

Chapter 19

Faith in Kona

In February 2012, my Masters swim team started swimming the 10 x 100s again. My times were consistently just above two minutes, which was faster than the previous year. It was just eight months until Kona, and I felt just as strong for each lap and was overjoyed with my progress!

I also started running in the winter running series at Hudson Gardens, which is a lush, botanical garden and historic landmark attraction near my house in Littleton. They offered three races: the 5K/10K in December, 5Mile/10M in January, and a 5M/10M in February, which were named the Santa Stampede, Frosty's Frozen, and the Snowman Stampede, respectively.

The Santa Stampede runs along the banks of the South Platte River in Littleton, Colorado, and when racers grace the finish line, steaming cups of hot cocoa await. Thousands of runners sign up for these events, which keep people focused on training during the long Colorado winter weather. Frosty's Frozen and the Snowman Stampede are flat races, beginning and finishing at Hudson Gardens. The Hudson Garden series is considered one of the best winter distance races in Colorado and it offered me a sense of community during the long winter months.

Even though these weren't considered "A" races, they kept me on track with training and helped me stay focused on going to Kona. In an athlete's season, you categorize races by A, B, C, or fun. A are the most important because they lead to your ultimate goal when you do well. B's are second most important, and then C's and fun races are just for fun. You identify all of these the year before your prime season, so Gretchen and I had identified them in 2011. I missed the first race due to a trip to New York, but I ran the distance of the race myself the week before and wasn't fast. I went out too fast, too early, and crashed and burned. I felt like I was choking during the run, which didn't impress Gretchen when I reported back to her.

Although I was excited at the start of the next race since I had such a strong warm-up, I went out too fast again. Gretchen instructed me to go at a 10k pace, but I blew up again around the 5-mile mark. I think I was running 8:25 and 8:15 miles at the beginning of the race. I had to walk for a little bit three different times just to get my breath back. I was able to pull it together to finish strong but didn't have anything left in the tank.

Gretchen still wasn't impressed. She told me that she was considered old and could run 7:45 miles. I felt terrible. I knew exactly what I needed to succeed, and it certainly wasn't Gretchen putting me down over my times. I told her I needed positive reinforcement, not negative feedback. I told her she had to give me some positive support sometimes instead of continually telling me what I was doing wrong. She was a good coach and did her part to be more positive. She told me I was her most consistent athlete, and that consistency would pay off.

In mid-February, I went to Orlando for seven days for an annual convention that Keller Williams calls "Family Reunion" because it's like getting together with your family. While there, I went for a 9.5-mile run that felt fantastic since the terrain was flat and at sea level. I didn't run again that week until the day before the last winter race, when I just did an easy run on the treadmill to loosen my muscles.

I returned to Denver to run the race, and found the 10 miles to be a muddy and somewhat snowy course. Gretchen was worried that I hadn't run enough, but

I assured her I was ready for the race. I had a solid warm-up and she suggested I start out slow and run a negative split (meaning the last half of the race is faster than the first) so I could finish strong. I decided to carry my own water, and this turned out to be a good idea since there were only two water stations despite the distance of the course.

After running for about 45 minutes, I reached the 5-mile mark. I thought it was good practice for racing. I went out a little too fast, but was still slower than I wanted to be. I ran 8:45 to 9 minute miles and felt good through the 5-mile mark. When I reached the 7 to 8 mile mark, my body blew up. I had to walk a short distance to recover and had a hard time maintaining my pace. The next miles I ran were 9:40-10:00, and once I reached the 9.5-mile mark, I reached into the tank and found a little strength and power left. I ended up averaging 8:48 minute miles, which was good for me for the distance. I would have been much happier with 8:30's, but either way my stamina and times were improving.

The surprising part was how sore my body was during the race. While I was running, my right hamstring and knee were sore. When I finished, I felt okay and cooled down properly and stretched. I came home, took a hot shower and stretched, then went to a real estate appointment. By the end of the appointment, my body ached. My left knee was the worst, and I didn't know why. I stayed in for the evening and propped my legs up hoping rest would let them recover.

KEY SIX

"NO" DISCIPLINE

Chapter 20

The Discipline to Say "No"

I was learning something new: the "No" Discipline. What I learned is sometimes it is important NOT to do things, especially while training. It's important not to succumb to distractions, like texts or Facebook, or to let your thoughts scatter. It's also important to NOT work out all the time and become addicted to the feeling of it. I was training hard for several hours every day, competing in races, improving my skills, and I was discovering the real discipline of saying "No" to things that would take me away from doing the things needed to accomplish my dream. I was noticing things beyond the texting, email and Facebook distractions. Things like becoming addicted to the drama or chaos of a situation, the attraction of "busy-ness", looking like I was essential to every situation, and being the hero who could solve every problem. These were things that I had done for a good part of my life, and now I was realizing that they were actually distracting me from what I was here to accomplish without providing real, tangible rewards.

And then there were the "emergencies." How many times had I let myself get off track by just taking care of that one "immediate" thing that I thought was an "emergency"? When I started saying no to these things, I realized that they were not really emergencies—just interruptions in the way of me ultimately accomplishing my dreams.

Saying "no" to distracting and disempowering thoughts was a huge step for me in my training. This really came into play at the Sterling Half Ironman Triathlon Series where the terrain, weather and other conditions were difficult and unpleasant. It would have been easy to entertain disempowering thoughts about all of that.

The Sterling HITS had been a race where "No" Discipline really served me. There were so many things about this race that could have really taken me out. I had to stay focused on the race itself, not on the sand, not on the heat, and certainly not on the boring landscape. Focusing on those things instead of doing what it took to just perform would have been disastrous for me. It would have also been easy to get lost in some diversion rather than keep my head in the race. But I did keep my head in the race by saying "No" to the diversions and distractions. I stayed focused on my water and nutrition, and I made it! I didn't need the intravenous fluids some of the others did at the finish line. I could have let myself be diverted by any number of things and gotten completely off my goal or, worse, just thrown in the towel. But I didn't. The uncomfortable running in the sand could have distracted me, but I stayed focused and kept myself from getting injured.

At the Cambridge race when I became aware that I was bored while waiting, I said, "No!" to the negative thoughts that came up. I took the opportunity to rewire my limiting beliefs and create empowering things to say to myself. I became excited by the energy of the crowd and the other athletes when the racing became dull for me. When I became sick to my stomach during the race, I said

"No" to stopping and did what I could with the nutrients I had with me. I kept going.

One of the big "No" Discipline elements of my training that actually came as a surprise to me was the month I had to take off training. It was important to NOT do the thing that I had been doing for so long so that my body and my brain could take a much-needed rest. This is so important in our lives: to make sure we have downtime where we take time off the activities we spend a lot of time in, even when we really love what we are doing. Your brain and body just need some time to do something different for a little while. This may be why people in some professions like teaching at the university level take sabbaticals. And it could be a key to why so many people begin to feel burned out, even in jobs they really love.

We even need to have "No" Discipline with some of the things we really love, like listening to music while training. Up to a certain point, I had always used my iPod in training and racing. I thought I needed music or some distraction. Then my coach Gretchen told me she never trained with one, even on long bike rides. She explained that athletes couldn't use them during the Ironman. The sooner I started to train without my iPod, the better—although I couldn't fathom how I would deal with how boring it could be to train without music.

I was dreading my first long run without my iPod, but it ended up opening my eyes. I was running near my house on the highline canal trail, a beautiful soft dirt trail that runs central Denver to south Denver and is lined with big, mature trees and lots of big beautiful homes. I could feel the soft dirt as my feet sank in a little as I ran. I enjoyed the trail because it was easy on my joints and made my real estate agent heart happy as I passed by the homes. Because of not having my iPod music drowning out my thoughts, I could think clearly and found that great thoughts just naturally bubbled up in my mind. My workouts became something I looked forward to as they rejuvenated my brain, though sometimes I wished I had a recording device with me because of the great ideas I came up with! I developed a keen ability to play songs at will, in their entirety, in my head. When I got sick of a song, I would just switch it in my head and start a new one, like it was playing on the radio.

It seemed I had an endless on-demand library of thoughts and ideas I was just now discovering and tapping into. Even though none of the books or articles I read talked about it, I realized how this would help me free and discipline my thoughts in every part of my life.

After that first run without the iPod, I realized I had been accustomed to having some sort of chatter or background noise going 24-7 throughout my life. Whether it was television or radio, something was always on, whether I was at home or at work. I never knew what a distraction it was until I admitted it must have been some sort of security blanket for me. I finally decided to leave it behind. Yes, I was leaving behind my "woobie", my pacifier, at the age of 43. When I gave up running with my iPod, I was able to deepen my spiritual relationship because my mind and soul were freer to talk with God.

This serenity, ability to focus on what was around me, and my deepening spiritual relationship really stood out when I finally competed in the Ironman World Championship in Kona. I paid attention to all the details—the sights, the sounds and how it felt to be there. I wasn't distracted by music, except for the songs I would play in my head. This "No" discipline of running without an iPod had totally altered my experience of what I was up to. Not to mention keeping my focus on things in the Sterling HITS where the sights and conditions weren't great at all, but paying attention to all of it was a contribution to my getting through the race without hurting myself.

Here is a list of some of the things I had to say no to during my training and racing:

- Working out all the time, because there is a tendency to think that more is better. More working out is not better. It's actually worse.
- Distractions like texting, Facebook, Instagram, email, and Twitter.
- Thoughts that weren't focused on what I had to do to achieve my dream.
- Negative thoughts like "I'm failing at this," "I'm going to fail," "This sucks."

• Runners high – you can get addicted to it. It feels good. And it can become a real addiction, just like a drug addiction. In fact, it's listed in the DSM, the official medical manual of psychological disorders.

• Getting addicted to the chaos of situations because they can make you feel like you're the rescuer or superwoman.

• Being the hero. When you feel physically great from working out every day, it's a huge validation of your abilities. You feel super-human, and can leap tall buildings. You feel like you can solve every problem. Even if that were true, and it's not, you don't have the time to solve every problem.

• Getting addicted to the chaos of a situation, drama or the busy-ness of things. It can look like further validation of your own importance. You might be thinking, "Oh, I have to do this, this, this…. I'm so busy, so important." Really it is all just ego. You have to tell yourself to get over yourself already! You're not the important part; achieving your goal, the thing you said is important, is the key.

• Allowing yourself to get off track by taking care of immediate things and interruptions.

Sometimes I found myself saying, "Oh, I forgot to do this thing," and it wouldn't be related to the current task at hand, the one that I was doing because it was focused on achieving my dream. Instead of taking out the 10 minutes to do it, I would jot down a note of what it was that I needed or wanted to do and put it in my schedule in the future when I had an opening. I would even build in windows of time in my schedule to slot those items into. It could be every day at 4:30, for example. I found that having a time-blocked schedule that supported my goal really made a difference in "No" Discipline!

Chapter 21

Accelerating My Biking Abilities

It was seven months to Kona, March 2012, and three months until my Kona Qualifying Race in Cambridge where I would demonstrate I was capable of competing at the Kona Ironman World Championship. My coach Gretchen had earlier announced to the team that she was planning a bike camp for one week in Las Vegas and had decided to rent out a house outside of Henderson that could host about 12 people. I was so excited at the prospect that I jumped at the opportunity and was the first person to sign up! I knew it would be a difficult part of training, and I focused on the fact that I would learn a lot about myself and get faster at cycling.

I started focusing on the logistics to get my tri bike and me there. I had named my red tri bike Chrissie after Chrissie Wellington, the Ironman World Championship female who always wore Red in Kona.

We only had a few options: drive yourself and your bike there, fly yourself and the bike, or fly and have someone else transport the bike. I had made the drive years before and swore I wouldn't do it again. I didn't relish the thought of taking my handlebars or the seat off for transport. I knew my limitations; I was not a good bike mechanic. I decided to try finding a bike transport and got names from others, including my coach and my bike mechanic.

However, nobody was going to Las Vegas. Gretchen's husband Tom jumped in and begged those driving to take as many bikes as they could for the flyers. A guy named Conor got in touch with me and said he could take my bike for a fee and a latte. I jumped at the offer. Meanwhile, I decided to improve as much as I could and looked forward to hearing more of the stories of other athletes at this event, especially those who were Ironman pros.

The weeklong bike camp in Henderson was set for triathletes, cyclists, and those training for the Ironman. Gretchen and Tom planned a daily bike route through Lake Mead State Park, swimming with a Master's program for three days, and running three to four days. The house they rented was about 12 miles from the entrance of the park and close to the pool. There were thirteen athletes and we all shared in cooking, cleaning, and training during the camp.

I had never been to a bike camp before, nor had I biked in Ride the Rockies, MS150, Triple Bypass, or any of the other big rides in Colorado. I was excited about participating in the bike camp but didn't know what to expect or how the week would go for me. I knew the camp would help my Ironman training and that I was in great hands. I had the assurances of my coaches, plus top-level athletes had said how beneficial it was for them.

I looked forward to a week away in a warm climate with more seasoned athletes. I was going to share a car rental and a room with a woman named Trish. Gretchen said we were similar level riders and that it would be good for us to get to know each other. We planned to meet at the Las Vegas airport and rent a car to make our way to the house.

We arrived in Nevada on a warm day. Trish and I met at baggage claim and swiftly got our bags, rented a car and made our way to the rental house. We were among the first athletes there so we made our way to our room and quickly unpacked all our gear. My training called for a run, so I got ready and headed out.

Training at sea level was fantastic. I felt like I could run forever, and I had lungs the size of Texas.

John and Conor arrived that night from Denver. John was a 30ish-year-old racer from Texas who was pursuing Ironman, and Conor was a 40ish-year-old Irishman living with his wife and children in the Tech Center area of Denver. He had completed Olympic distance races and was transitioning to the half Ironman. Many of the other athletes had already arrived, and among them were solid, fast athletes with a long list of marathons and Ironman distance triathlons under their belts.

The coaches put together a schedule that included the mileage and discipline for each day—including running, biking, and swimming, plus time for meal prep and cleanup. They went to Costco and bought a massive amount of food for the week. Even though the house they rented had six bedrooms and three baths, it had the smallest refrigerator known to humankind. Getting all the food crammed into it was a miracle!

The first day of camp, we went to the Masters swim at 5:30 a.m. It was still dark when we arrived at the massive heated pool. There must have been 20 or 30 lanes, and the saline concentration was higher than what I was used to in Colorado making water easier to swim in. We got changed and swam under the stars. The sun rose over the horizon during our workout, and it was absolutely beautiful.

Pool at Henderson Bike Camp

We went back "home" to a massive breakfast—every breakfast and dinner there was a healthy and delicious buffet—then we prepared for our ride.

We made our way to the Lake Mead park entrance and stopped to pay for the week. We reached the turnaround after 15 miles. Two girls asked me to take their picture, and I did, only to discover that everyone else took off, leaving me in last position. Here was a distraction that I should NOT have gotten involved in.

The wind presented an added challenge, but I was up for it. I pushed myself on the way back, but I couldn't catch up with the rest of the group and started to have knee pain. I caught up to Trish and Conor. Trish told me that she had ridden behind me and noticed that I was angling my knees on my pedal stroke, and that was probably causing my knee pain.

Karen celebrating at Henderson Bike Camp

Part of our course was also part of the Lake Las Vegas Half Ironman World Championship, which Gretchen competed in. Tom rode with me and taught me about maintaining a smooth, efficient, powerful stroke. He said to act like you are jamming your toes into the front of the shoe; then, on the downward part of the stroke, act as though you're cleaning mud off the bottom part of the shoe. When I concentrated on that, I was much faster and more powerful, especially going uphill. When we finished, we went back to the house to gorge ourselves on food and have recovery drinks before jumping in the pool. Now that's my kind of recovery!

We rode 40 miles that first day. Then the mileage increased about 10 miles a day to a high of 80 to 100 miles. We had a recovery day of 30 to 40 miles and then a mini-triathlon on the last day. That last day consisted of swimming in the morning, a 60-mile bike ride, and a 3- or 4-mile run.

The rest of the week was pretty much a repeat of the first day, except for a few nights when a pro Ironman athlete, Jesse, joined us for dinner. He took a month each year to train in Vegas at the beginning of his season. Jesse gave me some great advice about racing and reminded me to be honest with myself on race day. He suggested identifying how I felt on a scale of 1-10, 10 being high. He said women are better at this mental exercise than men because women's egos don't get in the way. If the number was a 7, for instance, then I should race the best possible way for a 7. Jesse told me athletes tend not to finish the race when they try to always race at a level 10, when they don't feel a true 10. I thought this was genius, and it changed my mindset about my progress and my racing.

Amazing things happened during that week. I found I could increase my mileage in biking, running, and swimming day after day, and my muscles continued to perform. My body rose to the challenge each day. Jesse told me this would happen if I let it. And he said that once the week was over, if I let my body recover I would be faster than I was before going to the camp. He was right! I also found that I was leading our group much of the time—though others did, as well—and it felt great.

I told Gretchen I was concerned about peaking too early in the season, since my Kona Qualifier race was not until June. She assured me there would still be plenty of work to get done in the coming months. I decided to trust her knowledge and continued putting everything that I had into getting to Kona.

Karen displaying her strength at Lake Mead - Henderson Bike Camp

During that week at camp, we biked 311 miles, swam for 3 miles, and ran 17 miles. I got to know twelve other athletes and had a great time with all of them. It was inspiring to be around people who were also looking to achieve things at a high level. I realized I could achieve more, go further, and race harder than I ever thought possible.

It was all about getting past my "mental governor"— the mechanism in the brain that tries to protect you from doing things that can hurt your body. The "mental governor" tends to kick in and talk you out of doing something when you're pushing your limits. It became obvious to me that the mental governor is what every athlete in the Ironman needed to confront and move past. That week, I learned how to get past mine.

HIT YOUR GOALS, ENJOY THE VICTORY& SET NEW GOALS, DREAM AGAIN

Chapter 22

Kona

Kona! Ironman World Championships.

Making preparations to go to Kona involved checking around a year before the race only to discover that all of the hotels and vacation rentals increased their rates during the Ironman and imposed a 10-day minimum stay. There were

50,000 people coming to the small area of Kona, who would pay these rates, and availability would be driven to nothing. The moment I got the lottery spot on April 15th, I communicated with Ruby and Crystal to schedule a meeting at the beginning of May to start planning and get the best possible prices by booking so early.

At that point, Ruby's friend Alicia, whom I had known for years, wanted to join us. Crystal said our mutual friend Marge wanted to come, too. This group of women came to be known as "the Sistas." The Sistas included my biological sister, Ruby; my best friend, Crystal; Ruby's longtime friend, Alicia; and Crystal's friend, and therefore mine, Marge. We're all right around 5'6" and we all look similar to each other. People even call Ruby and me twins because we both have the same small build, brown eyes, and short dark hair. In fact, we all have dark hair, with the exception of Marge who has short, blonde, spiky hair.

Alicia is a photography enthusiast, so she brought three cameras and took pictures of everything. I urged her on every step of the way. I felt so proud that she was documenting everything with as much or more enthusiasm as I would have. I will always love her for that.

All of these ladies have fantastic wits and keep me laughing incessantly. They are all very intelligent and wonderfully zany, each in her own way. Each possesses a larger heart than regular humans! They are the kind of people you can count on when you truly need a friend, when the going gets tough or the chips are down— no matter what. I was overjoyed to have all of them come to Kona and not only share in the experience, but make it more amazing by their sheer presence.

As I stood basking in the friendship of my Sistas, I thought fondly of two other dear longtime friends, Karen and Randy who visited Kona in October 2011 to get engaged. One day at work, I got a text from Karen inquiring about my shoe size. I thought it odd and sent back a question mark. I knew she was in Hawaii with Randy. Then the phone rang, and it was Randy, asking what my shoe size was. Still puzzled, I asked why he wanted to know. Turns out, they found an area where the Ironman World Championships had taken place just the weekend before and had discovered a ton of merchandise for sale. Karen remembered how badly I wanted but couldn't find online Ironman Kona merchandise. They had decided to go shopping for me and had found flip-flops that had the word

"Ironman" across the soles that I could use at the pool. I got so excited that I stood up from my desk and asked what else was in the store. Randy said there were lots of stores, all with large assortments of hats, shirts, gloves, swimsuits, and ball caps—everything imaginable and unimaginable with the Ironman word and logo. It was an Ironman paradise! I came to my senses and with gratitude said, "Whatever you want to get, I will love, because it will be from you." Not only did they get the flip-flops, they got me a hat and a red Ironman tribal shirt. I later had Craig Alexander and Mirinda Carfrae sign the hat in Cambridge. I put it on my nightstand so that I could see it every morning and night, just like Jack Canfield said he did in The Secret, to make his dream come true. Karen, who is very artsy, put together a mini-dream board of photos they took of the pier, the historic sign that marks the finish line, Alii drive, and the bay. At the bottom, she cut out letters to spell, "Karen is an Ironman." I cried when I saw the loving gifts they had made and purchased for me. I wore the flip-flops to the pool every day and took them to Kona with me. I put the mini-dream board up in my office so I could look at it many times throughout the day, visualizing myself there. Words can never adequately convey the gratitude I felt for them for helping me visualize being there.

When we arrived in Kona, Brandon helped me train and guided me through exercises to reduce the strain on my legs. He also had me practice alongside his athletes who were turning pro. One of them was competing and introduced me to every pro we came across. They helped me take in the entire experience without freaking out. Brandon was supportive at every breath and continuously asked me if I had more questions, making sure I had everything I needed. He made me feel like I was part of the group and that I belonged there, even among pros. My previous coach had always pointed out the chasm between my abilities and theirs, as though I was supposed to understand my place.

I felt at ease leading up to the Ironman. Because my hamstring and knee were feeling better, I felt confident and strong. I knew it was my time and that this was my destiny. I knew deep in my heart that everything was going to be great and that God was going to bring me the rest of the way, so in a way that was uncharacteristic for me, I wasn't worried. After arriving in Kona, I was calm and completely at peace with what I needed to do. I was ready to bring my dreams and goals to fruition. I thought I would be a bundle of nerves, but an overwhelming sense of belonging and peace came over me.

It was Tuesday night when we arrived at the condo. Ruby and I flew together, Crystal and Marge flew together, and Alicia came on her own. Ruby and I arrived on October 9th, the Tuesday before the race. Our route went from Denver to San Francisco to Kona, and I took pictures of lots of things along the way, like the departures monitor that showed our destination of Kona, HI. I wore a pink plastic lei around my neck and a white t-shirt that said, "If triathlon were easy, it would be called football." Ruby was really excited, too. She had never been to Hawaii before. After we flew over the Pacific Ocean for what seemed an eternity, we finally started seeing the Hawaiian Islands. As we got closer, we could see things that we knew from TV, like the Natural Energy Lab, the black lava fields and beaches, and the north tip of the island where the bike turn-around is. The more we recognized, the more excited we got! Finally, we landed at the open-air Kona airport, and were met by the smell of tropical flowers and the warmth and humidity on our skin as soon we exited the plane. We walked to baggage claim, taking in the palm trees, blue sky, and lush, green plants. Finally, we were here!

Ruby and I met Brandon on Wednesday at Kailua Bay where all of the Ironman athletes and my icons had started their championship journeys. I arrived there at 7:00 in the morning to do a 40-minute swim. I was surprised to see how small the area was in comparison to how it had looked on television. I was absolutely mesmerized to be in this bay and enjoyed every moment of taking it all in. I was finally here!

Ironman banners hung along the waterfront. The water was crystal-clear blue with gorgeous coral and abundant sea life. It was easy for me to turn my focus to the beauty instead of concentrating on swimming. Before I got in the water, I saw several people I knew from Colorado, and they suggested I put on Bodyglide to counteract chafing from the salt water. I didn't have any, but made a note to remember it the next day. We met several people, including quite a few from other countries, and it was interesting to hear all the different languages.

As Brandon led me through all the people, we joined his other two athletes to get ready to go in the water. We introduced ourselves and talked about the recent races we had done to get here. Then, magic happened! Chris McCormack—a pro and two-time world champion—walked up behind me. Brandon called out to him using a funny name. Chris came over and gave him a hard time in his great Aussie accent. He and Brandon knew each other from having trained together in Boulder and knowing the same pro athletes. Brandon introduced all of us as his athletes, and Chris acknowledged us and wished us luck for race day. WOW! Instead of feeling star-struck, like a celebrity groupie, I felt I belonged here. I was accepted. I had not had that sense before, and I couldn't thank Brandon enough for it.

There were quite a few people in the water when I went in, so I tried to pay attention to avoid colliding with anyone. The water was a bit cold, but I acclimated quickly and felt like I got into a good stroke. My stroke was no longer taking me off course. When I started swimming, I realized I hadn't stretched my shoulders before beginning. I felt fine, so I continued. I started seeing the other swimmers and made my way down a clear path to the buoys. I let a lot of water flow through my mouth, and the salt water made my mouth feel raw. The waves did not affect me except for when I sighted, so I needed to adjust my timing. It felt like I was swimming fast, and I felt buoyant in the water.

We swam out to the fourth orange buoy, about 1,500 yards or so, and turned back. There was a floating island and a red boat with several long-boarders out past the buoy turnaround. It was a fun atmosphere, and as I swam back and got out, I felt happy and content that I had just swum in the same bay as my icons. They would soon become my forerunners, rather than icons. This was where I would start the race and realize my dream.

The Ironman team was setting up the race area, and it was soon filled with tents, inflatables, and fencing. I found Ruby and told her how my swim went. I talked with Brandon a bit, and he shared some more with me about how the swim course would be set up. His guidance helped me feel more confident about the swimming portion of the race.

Ruby and I went for coffee at a place across the street from the King Kamemeha Hotel, named after the boy king of the island. It was smaller than it had looked on television. After our coffee, I headed over to pick up my race packet at 10 a.m. The process to get the packets was well organized. Only athletes, no family or friends, could go in, so it moved faster. Volunteers stood at the entrance to welcome athletes, and they asked questions from genuine interest in the athletes' stories. Many of the volunteers knew of the city of Boulder and wanted to talk about it, and one woman noticed the Ironman logo on my fingernails. I had taken in a swim bag with the Ironman logo on it to the nail shop and asked the nail techs if they could re-create it on my thumbnails. After several conversations among themselves on how they might do it, they drew it on and filled it in. I could tell they thought it was ugly, but I was proud!

When I approached the check-in table, I started by finding my name and race number on the list and then confirmed I was a current USAT member. I signed a medical waiver and liability agreement. When they handed me my packet, it seemed small, considering everything that was needed for the race. They put a plastic wristband around my wrist and scanned the packet, which beeped to prove the timing chip was working.

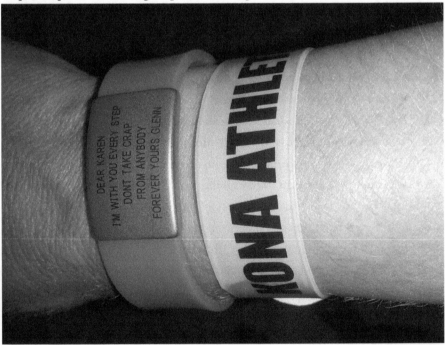

Kona Athlete and Glenn's gift armbands for the big race

I was also wearing my red Road ID bracelet gift from Glenn, in the captioned photo. Distance athletes order these from Road ID so that if you get in a crash and become unconscious, your ID bracelet tells who you are and gives an emergency contact name and phone. Glenn ordered one for me, and he knew I was superstitious that having emergency contact information on my wrist might somehow "invite" an accident. So he ordered it to read: "Dear Karen, I'm with you every step. Don't take crap from anybody. Forever yours, Glenn."

The organizers handed me a beautiful Ironman World Championship backpack with a plastic ID that contained a schedule of events on the back. I almost cried from the excitement! It was like a dream as I went through the process, and I was enjoying every minute. I went outside and showed Ruby everything, and she took pictures of me with my bag, wristband, and ID. It was so wonderful to be sharing this experience with her, and I am forever grateful that she took the time to be there for me.

My bike was delivered to the expo area the next day, Thursday. Ruby and

Kona athlete packet contents

Crystal went with me to pick it up. After I put the pedals on and changed into riding gear for a short training ride, they went back to the condo with my gear bag. It was exciting to ride out to the Energy Lab because it was one of the magical areas the Ironman announcer always talked about during the race. The Natural Energy Laboratory of Hawaii Authority, located 7.3 miles from the finish line, has as its mission to develop and diversify the Hawaiian economy by providing resources and facilities for energy and ocean-related research, education, and commerce, in an environmentally sound and culturally sensitive manner.

Meanwhile, Crystal and Ruby walked around the Expo seeing all the swag vendors and doing their best to rub elbows with the celebrities of the race. They scored a great pink visor from Infinit with Kona 2012 stitched on it by telling them I was racing and using their product. They proudly gave it to me when I returned to the condo, and it instantly became my favorite.

Thursday was also the day of the pre-race athlete dinner. Athlete families were invited, so Ruby and Alicia went with me since the other three Sistas hadn't arrived yet. The dinner was your average carb-loading, feeding-an-army fare, but the cool part was seeing all of the pomp, circumstance and heritage come alive. The dinner was held at the King Kamehameha Hotel rear parking lot. A big stage had been set up with a tall backdrop and jumbotrons so everyone in the 4,000-person audience could see. Round, 10-person tables were in the immediate front for the pros and VIPs. After that were long tables that sat 20 people per side—all white with white plastic folding chairs. Enormous food tables were set up on each side of the crowd, with horse-troughs full of ice and water, Gatorade, soda pop, etc. It was a beautiful night. It was 78 degrees, 40% humidity, and that lovely Hawaiian trade wind gently blew the palm trees that lined the edge of the King Kam property. The dinner would start at 6:30, and I was so excited that I felt nervous with an overabundance of energy. This program would kick off the officialdom of the race for me, and I was taking it all in like a sponge, wanting to savor every moment, every feeling, every memory. I felt truly joyful and grateful to be there.

The Ironman announcer, Mike Reilly, emceed the event and spotlighted none other than Julie Moss and Kathleen McCartney. They were, fittingly, being inducted into the Ironman Hall of Fame before the race day that would commemorate the 30-year anniversary of the historic race. Also highlighted were the youngest and oldest athletes racing. Among the men, the oldest competitor was one of my favorites, Lew Hollander, 83 years young and in his 22nd consecutive year at Kona. Man alive, what it takes to do that! The oldest female was Sister Mary Buder, 78 years young and a Catholic nun who had competed in other Ironmans. I was awestruck by both of them, and we all stood to acknowledge their accomplishments and show our respect to those standing on the stage.

I had the chance to reconnect with Tyla, the athlete I had raced with in Cambridge where she had taken first in her age group for a slot. We said hello and shared our take on things thus far. She asked me how I was getting to the start line on race morning, and it was right then I realized I didn't have a plan for it! She said her parents (whom I had met when we all stayed at the same place in Cambridge) were going to drop her off and could come by and pick me up, as well. I gratefully accepted, and we pinned down a time.

We all continued posing for photos for Alicia. Her favorite pose involved standing with one arm drawn back by your ear and the other extended straight, angled toward the sky and looking up at your hand. She said it reminded her of Greek gods and the greatest athletes from Greek mythology. Ruby and I thought it fitting and went along with it, laughing.

Karen & Team Sistas striking a pose

Photo of condo flowers

On Friday, I biked from the condo 15 miles south and back. Then ran 1.5 miles from the condo into town. Then, Ruby took my swim stuff to meet me at the pier for a swim. During my bike ride, I saw Chrissie Wellington with Craig Alexander, and I was so excited I just about crashed! The road on my run was crowded with pedestrians and cars. Some 50,000 people had descended on a five-mile area for the Ironman. The air was electric with energy.

At 3:30 p.m., I met up with one of Brandon's other athletes, and we went together to drop off our gear in the transition area. Brandon told me it would be a neat experience, and boy, was he right! Gear drop takes place the afternoon before the race. You take all of your gear for biking and running to the transition area to set it up and leave for the night so it's there and ready to go on race morning. For full Ironman races, you get two gear bags and two special needs bags. Of the two gear bags you use, one is for all of your biking gear (helmet, sunglasses, cooling sleeves, socks, and shoes—unless they are clipped into your pedals like the pros), and the other is for all of your run stuff. These get placed on racks with hooks for each one in numerical race number order, so that you can run through the gear bag area, pick up your bag quickly, then go to the transition tent to put all your gear on. Ruby and the Sistas came with me to see all of it. The transition area was for athletes only, so they had to wait for me outside. All the race fencing had been set up, so we athletes formed a single file line, feeding into one "lane" through the fencing, taking us into the transition area right next to the King Kamehameha Hotel.

As soon as we got in line, we turned a corner leading into the transition area, where a volunteer assisted each of us individually. On the outside of the fence, people sat in folding chairs with yellow legal pads and wrote down every single type of equipment we used. Figuring we all had our best race gear, these people were from equipment and product companies, taking down statistics about who used what. Sometimes, they would ask what brand of bike saddle we used if they couldn't readily see it. This was absolutely surreal. I felt like a celebrity walking down a red carpet. At first, I didn't know what they were doing because they weren't looking at the athletes' faces at all. They just kept their eyes forward and wrote furiously as we filed by. When Grant (Brandon's other athlete) enlightened me, I had about 15 feet remaining to take it all in and bask in the experience.

Once in transition, a race volunteer named Becky met me. She had short brown hair, glasses, and looked to be in her early fifties. She welcomed me with a smile and asked if it was my first time at Kona. I proudly said yes and that it had been my lifelong dream. She said she would spare me no part of the whole experience. Another volunteer came up and put a small orange and blue sticker on my bike with the MDot logo (a large block-style "M" with a dot above the middle of it like an "I"), showing that my bike was officially allowed to be in the transition area. I was already thrilled and excited, and we hadn't even moved!

Becky took me to my bike's assigned position in the racks. Some $40 million of bikes were fit carefully onto the pier. It was a sight to see! Since this was the World Championships, there were some very nice (and expensive) triathlon bikes, one for each of the 2,000 competitors. They were lined up in long rows, very close together, so all of them fit on the small pier. All of the bright paint colors glistened in the sun, and it looked like one of those dot paintings where you can see another image in it. We set my bike in its place, with my helmet, sunglasses, water and gel bottles (I would fill those the next morning). We made sure my tires were properly inflated, leaving a bit of room for expansion due to the humidity. Becky pointed out helpful markers to look for to locate my bike quickly the next day. Then she took me through the route I would take to and from my bike and the spot where I would leave for the run. It was all clear and well thought out.

From there, she took me to the area where my gear bags would be: one for biking and one for running gear. There were different colored plastic drawstring bags that went into two different areas, all laid out perfectly so that they could move 2,000 athletes around ultra-efficiently on the small pier. At each location, she had me make sure everything I needed was in my bag, because the next time I would see it, I would be racing! With each drop, she had me line up the location of my bag from where I would approach that area.

She took me to the point where I would exit the bay after the swim and had me immediately turn left to go into the showers, which were in a covered pavilion-like structure with what looked like cut-off garden hoses hanging from the top. Fresh water would be running from the evenly laid out hoses, every three feet or so. The theory was that I would run up the stairs from the bay, pick a "line" of hoses, and just run through while peeling down my speed suit—a sleeveless, all-in-one, mid-thigh, non-buoyant suit with a back zipper like a wet suit. By being one continuous suit, it cuts down on drag that happens when you swim in a swimsuit or tri-kit. It has to be textile and non-buoyant, but it fits pretty tight so it has a bit of a compression quality to it. You wear your tri kit under it so you can unzip it and peel it off in one effort as you run through the shower of cold water on your way to your gear bag and the transition area. What a genius plan, I thought! I had never seen that at another race.

Then we went into the women's transition tent. It was nothing like I had imagined. It was approximately 20 feet long and 15 feet wide, with one row of back-to-back folding chairs in the middle and 6-foot folding tables on two sides of the perimeter. The other two sides had women-specific port-o-potties! I was dumbstruck. I stared at them and Becky said, "Now, when you exit the water, you will run through the shower and line yourself up with your bike gear bag in the tent that precedes this one. Then you will come in here and sit down in the chair. We will take the bag, and as you call out each item you want, we will hand it to you."

I queried, "I don't just put on all my stuff myself after grabbing it out of my bag?"

She said, "No. It's faster if you call it out and we hand it to you while you sit in this chair." Again, genius! Then she said, "Now, you can't pee in these chairs. If you have to go to the bathroom, you have to use the port-o-potty." I sat there looking at her, and managed to nod my head yes, indicating I had heard her.

She was about to move on to the next thing. I interrupted and said, "So, I'm guessing you tell me that because you mean the pros do it, right? " She nodded yes. I thought, That is so not my game here; I would never think of peeing in a chair to shave a minute off the clock. But then again, I'm not getting paid to be here like they are and don't have everything hinging on winning. For me, it was a glimpse into their world and a minuscule yet important insight into what it was like to be a pro under the pressures of the clock. Their life and their tactics on race day were totally different from mine. I do not live in that kind of a life during the race, nor do I experience the level of competition that they do.

I was caught up in thinking about what else it was like for the pros, when Becky said, "Okay, that's it. We will see you tomorrow." I didn't want this part of the experience to be over, so I asked her to verbally walk me through everything one more time, which she kindly did. I asked if she had done this before because she was good at it and completely calming and reassuring, and she said she had. She explained that there were 3,400 volunteers for the race. The most experienced ones could pick where they wanted to be and she loved being in the transition area where all the excitement was. I thought to myself, When I can't race anymore, that is what I will do, too!

With that breathtaking experience under my belt, I walked back to the area where we would hang out in the morning before starting the swim. It was on the bay side of the King Kamehameha Hotel where there were some grassy areas, sand, palm trees, gazebos, and pathways. A sacred, historic house that was roped off from the public, it was completely serene there and utterly quiet, even though it was just 500 yards from all of the chaos of the transition/start/finish area. I thought it looked like a tranquil place to ready myself mentally while waiting for the swim start. On the way from that area to transition, there was a swim gear bag table where they would take anything you took off before the swim, put it in another, differently colored drawstring plastic bag, and give it back to you post-race. Apparently, after the athletes took off, this would be converted to the post-race area. Where we started, we would finish. They would change this area into the place where they brought all the finishers to give them the coveted finisher medals, provide food, and take photos. I thought, Well, in just hours I will be back here, having completed my goal, and reflecting back on what was 30 years in the making. It was absolutely magical.

I came out of the transition process and saw the Sistas waiting for me. I must have had a spacey smile on my face because they immediately asked what had happened. I proceeded to tell them every detail and reveled in sharing it with them as we made our way back to the condo for dinner and an early bedtime.

I always have pasta with light tomato sauce, plain salmon, and bread the night before a race. It seems to digest well and give me energy the next day. I ate my dinner while everyone was doing their thing for dinner, having this or that and watching television. Next I went through my gear one last time, did some stretching, and made final preparations. I came out of the bedroom to find that the Sistas had put on matching bright orange t-shirts and red ball caps as team support for all of us. The shirts had black lettering on the front that said, TEAM KAREN, DENVER, CO, KONA 2012. On the back it said, OUR SISTA ROCKS! My shirt was different and said MY SISTAS GOT MY BACK. I was speechless and felt the tears coming on. We all put them on and gathered for a photo, taking on Alicia's crazy, Greek pose. I had brought beautifully colored hand-made greeting cards for each of them, and had written a special message to each one thanking them for sharing this special journey. It's safe to say there were plenty of hugs, kisses, tears, and excitement for the next day! We discussed the logistics of how we would meet up before the race so I could hand off the last things, like my cell phone. With that, I went to bed, and they weren't too far behind me.

October 13, 2012: Ironman Day!

I slept well that night and woke up at 3:45 a.m. so I could get picked up at 4:45 to get my body marked. I was brimming with excitement and butterflies. I had seen this on TV for 30 years, countless other athletes getting their race number in body marking, and now it was my turn! I felt so proud and cool, like

I had finally arrived. I showered, stretched, took my vitamins, prepared bread with peanut butter, got everything out of the fridge I needed for the day, took my watch from the computer charger, and gathered my things. I had already put my timing chip on the night before. I felt peaceful and excited as I prepared. I took my stuff out front where Tyla and her parents had just driven up to pick me up. Off we went. It was dark outside and fairly quiet on our way down Alii Drive to the start. From a ways away you could see the finish line tower and lights, and we both gasped in excitement upon seeing it. Alii Drive is a famous road that runs beside the Kailua Bay and ends at the finish line of the race. It is the final stretch of the finishers run that is always shown on TV, with 50,000 fans lining the white fencing barricades that follow the race course, squished three, four or five deep in places.

We got out of the car with our stuff and started walking the rest of the way to the north side of the King Kamehameha Hotel for body marking and to drop off our special needs bags. These were two more color-coded plastic drawstring bags that were transported to the halfway point of the bike and run leg for each athlete. I never saw the pros use these and had only heard them talk about it once, so I didn't quite understand what they were. Basically, you put anything you might need in the bag as a precaution, and you can use it at the halfway point. My brilliant sister thought of putting some Rockstar in an empty Gatorade bottle wrapped in foil, and we put in other things like Pepto-Bismol, Imodium, Aleve, gels, socks, etc. In the run special-needs bag, we put a headlamp because I had seen so many athletes running in the dark and falling, along with a fresh pair of shoes and socks, Vaseline for blisters, more Aleve and gels, and sodium to replenish my fuel belt. A fuel belt is an elastic belt that has a system to affix your race number bib on the front and then elastic loops to hold energy gels. It's for those athletes who want to carry their own, instead of using what they give out on the course. All these bags have your race number and name on them (pre-printed, no applying stickers like in other races) and then they are placed in the Energy Lab (and Hawi, for the bike leg) for you. It would be absolutely glorious, getting there and having that bag. They also provided seating at the Energy Lab in the run so athletes can sit down and go through the bag and change their shoes and socks if they needed to. The reason you don't hear about these bags is the pros never actually stop to go through their bag. They grab it on the fly, get out what they want while they are biking or running, then throw it to the side, like water cups at a marathon.

Tyla and I threw our special needs bags into the transport trucks and went to the tents for body marking. We flew through because it wasn't busy yet, and we had time to take photos for each other. We wanted to see some pros, but they were in another tent, and we didn't want to be delayed. We moved on to the tent where doctors check your weight and heart rate and do a quick once-over. They had smocks that had the MDot logo and said "Dr. Ironman"! They asked me to step on the scale to get a starting weight and explained I would be weighed again at the finish to see if any medical attention needed to be administered due to excessive body weight loss. Then they asked questions to assess if I was feeling strong, healthy and generally good. They wanted to know if I had any medical conditions or anything else they needed to know about.

Next, we were shuffled to the back of the hotel and the transition area. It was still dark, so they had huge lights up to illuminate everything. It was early, so I went over to my bike to check that everything was as it should be, and it was. Chrissie looked great and was ready to go. I had two large bottles of water, and I filled the handlebar water container and placed my plastic flask full of watered-down gels and my insulated bottle filled with Infinit and sodium mixture in the two basket cages.

I had read in Chrissie Wellington's book that she wrote sayings and meaningful words on her water bottles with Sharpies, so I had done the same. I wrote things like: Never, ever, ever give up (which was her favorite, and resonated with me); faith; Rich Roll; believe; 40% (referring to the proven fact that when you feel like you have nothing left, your body is only at 40 percent of its max); epic 5 (a race Rich Roll and his buddy, Jason, created for themselves, basically consisting of five Ironmans in five days on each Hawaiian island); and many other things that had become meaningful to me over the previous two years.

I was feeling so calm. I didn't have my usual pre-race jitters and had more time than I was used to. I decided to walk over to where the pros had their bikes. On my way, I passed Julie Moss and Kathleen McCartney readying their bikes. I felt like this was totally meant to be, and I wished them a great race. I could have stopped Julie and bothered her with my story of watching her 30 years ago, but I thought, *She probably hears that all the time and the last thing she wants is to be reminded today of that day.* It felt good just to see the two of them before the race.

I made my way over to where the pros had their bikes. Many of them were doing their preparations. I was so close to them, I could have reached out and touched them. I saw that almost all of them had on headphones, not just to listen to, but also to not be disturbed. I thought, *They are just like us,* having to get their stuff ready, and they have far more pressure to perform. I took a photo of Craig Alexander's rear end, because I had an opportunity to be this close to him. Why not? I thought he was sexy!

I looked at my watch and realized I should pass my phone to Crystal and officially put myself in race mode. I walked to the front of the King Kamehameha where team Sistas were waiting in their bright orange shirts. As I told them what I had seen, they smiled and completely understood how meaningful the morning had already been. I gave Crystal my phone and pointed out the numbers for Glenn and other people important to me so she could update them during the race.

At that point, Glenn and I had maintained a long friendship that was safe and wonderful. We could tell each other anything, including our innermost secrets. When I was on my road to Kona, we each were going through second divorces (in 2012) and figuring out our relationship with one another. Our deep, yet undefined, "official" connection added another layer of challenge and support at the same time.

With all of the Sistas standing around me, I teared up. They all meant so much to me. I couldn't have gotten here without them, and now I wouldn't see them again until the finish, several hours later. They saw me start to cry, and each one came in for a hug, telling me how great it was going to be and that it would be a magnificent day.

I left the Sistas and walked back to do a quick warm-up and put on my speed suit. I saw Chrissie Wellington saying hello to everyone and wishing them a good race. I also saw Sister Mary Buder and stopped to wish her well in her race and adding how I wanted to be racing at her age. She stopped everything and blessed me! I knew right then everything was going to be wonderful. I hugged her and went to stretch out a bit on the grass. I turned on my iPod and these songs came on in this order: "Tonight's Gonna be a Good Night," "Hold Your Head Up," and finally, "Get this Party Started." They were the perfect songs to hear before the race. I turned off my iPod and asked a fellow athlete next to me to spray my Bodyglide in places I couldn't reach. He did, and we talked briefly and then each got back into our mental zones. Now it was time to walk over to the bay and line up. Butterflies started swirling in my belly, but I didn't let them get to me. I felt excited but not scared at all. The small entry to the bay was packed and we were herded through the small opening to the stairs.

As I walked down to the water, I made a decision to enjoy every moment of the day and not be a slave to the clock. I figured that if I was looking at my watch all the time, I would miss the joy and beauty, and the whole day would pass me by. I realized I could rely on the fact that I was here and everything was going to go well. I had had this dream for so long that, just like a wedding day, I didn't want it to go by in a flash. I wanted to savor each delicious morsel of my Kona experience. I felt a big wave of relief come over me as I continued to make my way into the water to find my starting position.

Looking down, I was surrounded by athletes in pink and blue caps. I made my way to the water and saw Lew Hollander. I told him he was my role model and that I was happy to race with him. He sort of smiled at me, but he was already in his zone, so I left him and went to the seawall side of the bay. I pulled my cap down over my ears and my goggles into place, secured my nose-clip, and tested my goggles. I adjusted them a few times until they sealed and I started to warm up. Time passed too fast. I realized it was time to line up. I started to swim out to the line. I looked back and saw there were a ton of racers on the beach. I started worrying I was too far out and they would all swim over me. I grabbed onto a kayak to wait until the race started. I looked to find the Sistas and thought I could see them, so I waved to them.

Swimmers at the start — Kona

It had been my biggest thrill to think of hearing the cannon go off, signaling the start of the race. I had watched it on TV for 30 years. They always showed a close-up of it to honor John Collins, who founded the Ironman. A perfect smoke ring at the start of the race floated over the bay and the competitors as they started their swim. With the sun coming up to the east, the clear blue ocean, the brightly colored swim caps and clothes of all of the spectators, it was indelibly etched into my mind as the quintessential picture of the Ironman start. I even made Ruby promise to photograph it for me so I could see it later. It seemed like an eternity waiting for the start. My heart was pounding with anticipation and I was raring to go!

I was thinking about what it took to get here: everything I had done in training, in spirit, in faith and belief, and all the seeming missteps that had delivered me here—all because I had a dream and followed it. I felt relief that the day was here and a sense of enormity that I had hours of performance ahead of me, and I quickly changed to gratitude for getting to spend all of those hours in this beautiful, magical, sacred place. It was also suspenseful because I didn't know what the day might bring. At the same time, I was not worried about it at all. I was peacefully excited. The announcer's voice yelled over the noise of the crowd, "Go! Go! Go!" I was so caught off-guard and discombobulated that it took a minute to register what had happened, and then I started swimming. (I found out later that the cannon had malfunctioned. Crystal said that it went off about 8 seconds after we started.) I stuck my head in the water and started my strokes. The water was clear, rich, deep blue, and warm. It was smooth, and there were no waves to speak of.

The start was easier than I thought it would be, especially after being beaten up at plenty of other races and expecting this to be way worse. You get beaten up because of the large number of competitors with two arms, two elbows and two legs that are all moving into their swim stroke at the same time in a confined area. So everyone gets elbowed and kicked and your hand hits other athletes in all sorts of places as each person jostles to find their pace and position in the water. The bay opened up so quickly and the fast swimmers took off immediately, which allowed age groupers like me to spread out a bit, making the start easier than for any other race I had competed in.

The water was clear enough that I could see the paddleboards and boats under the water. There were many of them, and they were perfectly lined up leading to each buoy! This made sighting virtually unnecessary. All I had to do was make sure I could see them underwater and follow their line. What a glorious way to do it. I wished all races were like that!

I started thinking I should find an athlete to draft off. I swam over to some folks, but couldn't seem to get in their rhythm. Then, about a fourth of the way into the race, I felt someone drafting off of me. I thought I would shake this athlete like others had shaken me, but I just couldn't do it. They hung on and on and it felt like I was towing them, they were so close. I realized it would take more energy to try to shake them, so I kept going at my own pace until finally, they dropped off. The thought crossed my mind that this was going to be the easiest part of the race and I should relax and enjoy the enormous beauty. It was the most comfortable I had ever felt swimming.

After I went through the turn and headed back to the bay, I was breathing to my right and kept seeing this architecturally distinctive hotel on the opposite shore, called The Royal Kona. As I kept swimming, the hotel seemed to stay in

Swimmers in action — Kona

the same line with me. At one point I got mad, thinking it was following me or I wasn't moving! That experience made the last part of the swim seem long, but I kept going and thought about swimming as fast and smoothly as I could to be sure I beat the cutoff time.

As I wondered what time had elapsed and how close I was to the cutoff, I remembered the story of a paraplegic athlete who had missed the cutoff by seven seconds, two years earlier. He finished the swim and he was absolutely devastated when they told him as they helped him up the steps. I had cried for him when I saw it and I thought, There is no way I am going to miss this cutoff. I have come too far and worked too hard to miss this. That strengthened my resolve and I powered through to the end. Once I could see the familiar land and shore, I stood up and ran toward the volunteers helping athletes out of the water.

Karen leaving the water — Kona

I glanced down at my watch and saw my time: 1:52. I made the cutoff, which is 2 hours and 20 minutes! I beamed as I ran up the stairs. I ran through the showers and through the gear bag tent, grabbing mine quickly. When I entered the transition tent, the volunteer grabbed my bag and sat me down in a chair. By this time, I had my speed suit off, which revealed my racing kit (black, and red, with white tropical flowers, a KW logo and an ambigram spelling "faith" on the front bottom). The volunteer handed me a towel to wipe off the water on my skin from the swim and shower. I then called out for my socks, shoes, headband, and cooling sleeves. Another volunteer put sunscreen on my face, arms, legs, and hands and asked me what else I wanted. I said, "Well, what else do you have?" She said, "Vaseline, Chapstick, Bonk Breakers, gels, and Powerade." It was like a transition tent buffet!

The volunteer handed me my race belt with my number on it as the final item in my bag, signaling I should leave the tent and get out on my bike. I thought, Wow, this place is like a palace. I don't want to leave. I used the port-o-potty quickly and ran through transition to the area of the pier where my bike was racked. Chrissie's bright red color was shining in the sun and she was ready to go! My bike was one of the only bikes left in transition, but I reminded myself that I had decided to do my own race and take in every second and not worry as much about the time. I wanted to focus on the whole experience.

Out on the bike, everyone was cheering from the sidelines. I saw the Sistas, who had told the announcer, Mike Reilly, my story. When I passed by, he said, "There goes Karen Brown from Littleton, Colorado, whose Sistas came with her to support her and have her back." I was utterly shocked that he was talking about me. I felt special as I heard him continue, "We wish you well, Karen Brown." I zigged and zagged down a couple streets, making my way to the Queen K Highway. Queen Ka'ahumanu "the feathered mantle" (1768-1832) was queen consort and also regent of the Kingdom of Hawaii. She was the favorite wife of King Kamehameha I and the most politically powerful. Called "the Queen K" by the athletes, this is the famous stretch of highway for the entire bike leg and 7.3 miles of the run portion of the race. It is a stretch of black asphalt that seems to go on further than the eye can see.

It all hit me. I was in Kona. I was fulfilling my dream. It was all happening, just as I had visualized. I was proud to have beaten the cutoff time by such a nice margin. I pumped my fist in the air in victory, thinking of my former coach, Gretchen, who had said she didn't think I would make it. I thought of all of the naysayers I had come across along the way. I was in Kona and they weren't. Suddenly, I started crying in relief that I had triumphed. I enjoyed the moment and then collected myself, saying, All right, there's a lot more work to do here, get on it. With that, I put my arms and head down on my aero bars and started to cruise down the beautiful Queen K.

There were still quite a few people lining the highway, but the crowds diminished as I went further. I felt like I was biking alone, even though there were people in groups along the way. It was hot out and not too windy. I looked at the fields of black lava to my right. Volcanic eruptions eons ago had formed the Hawaiian Islands. What remains today is this beautiful hardened black lava rock, which is a stark contrast to the green grass, palm trees, and blue ocean. I find it breathtakingly beautiful. I started to notice all of the white rocks inscribed with sayings and couples' names and such. At first, I ignored them, wanting to focus on my bike cadence, speed, and nutrition intervals. When I got comfortable with that, I tried to read every saying—being careful not to affect my aero position—to keep my mind sharp and working on something. As I passed the rocks, I wondered who had put them there and why. I wondered if they painted the rocks, how many were needed, and how difficult it was to get them out there. These were the types of things I thought about when I had a lot of time on my hands competing in races.

When I was 25 percent of the way through the course, I looked at my watch. The pros would be passing the other way soon on the last half of their bike leg. I was still in the lava fields, and now there were also entrances to swanky resorts that were situated on the ocean. I started to see more spectators, and I asked who was leading. I didn't hear the answer because I was going by too fast. I started seeing the helicopters hovering, which meant the pros were close. The helicopters always follow them. I saw some of the men, but no one I recognized. It was a while before I saw the women. I saw Rini (Mirinda Carfrae) in pack two or three, but still nobody could answer who was leading. It seemed the pros were working hard to go that fast, which made me feel better.

After a while, I came to some hills. I continued to take in the scenery of the ocean on the left and the lava fields on the right. The landscape changed to orange as I made my way through a port of entry town called Kawaihae Harbor on my way to the bike turnaround point at Hawi. Two crosswinds hit me, each with a large gust, and then they never came again. I was relieved. Over the years, I had seen on TV athletes getting blown off their bikes by these infamous crosswinds. The road was a steady incline, and I noticed clouds rolling in as the skies grayed. I said something to a fellow racer about how it looked like weather

Karen on the biking leg — Kona

ahead. He bristled back, "Yeah, just what we need on top of having to climb these hills." This was someone who I had seen complete this race on TV, and I wondered how his negativity could help him. I brushed it off as I passed him and said, "Hey, great job and good luck." He didn't wish me luck back.

I was at home climbing hills. They had always been my favorite part of mountain biking and I loved them in road cycling, too. I settled in for more of it and hoped the weather would hold, but it didn't. It became progressively worse and by the time I reached Hawi, a downpour with driving winds made it difficult to see through my glasses. It seemed to take a long time once I crested the 54 miles uphill to arrive at the quaint fishing village known as Hawi. The television coverage had made it look like it was nearby, and it clearly wasn't. I passed what looked to be a suburban woman wearing an A-line below-the-knee skirt, sensible/popular rubber sandals, a rain jacket with a big Asian umbrella, and blonde shoulder-length straight hair. She was standing in the middle of the road, holding out a tray of prepared fish, offering it to me. I was totally caught off-guard and didn't say anything until I was past her. How weird, I thought. I had never seen that in a race.

Finally, the road leveled out and I could see charming little shops and the fencing that was at the bike turnaround. This was the official halfway point. The special needs bags were laid out in numerical sequence on the grass in a park after the turnaround. Volunteers started calling out my number as soon as they could see it so that the other volunteers down the line could grab my bag and hand it off to me. A young man handed me my bag. The rain and wind had stopped and the clouds were clearing. I was never so happy to see a can of Rockstar! I drank half of it in one gulp. I had been thinking about it ever since the turn at Kawaihae. I was a bit hungry and asked the volunteer if there were any Bonk Breaker bars available. Food isn't typically packed in the special needs bag, and I hadn't thought to pack any. I was on track with my Infinit and switched out the empty bottle for the new.

A lovely married couple heard my request and sprang into action. In their late forties, they had big, colorful umbrellas. She wore jeans and he, khakis, and they both sported Hawaiian print shirts and tennis shoes. They were as sweet as could be as they began looking through the bags of athletes who had already been through, hoping to find me a bar or two. They found some. However, they weren't bars I was used to, and I was concerned about stomach upset so I declined them. They were accommodating and asked how my race was going. They said they volunteered every year, it was usually rainy in that area, and all the athletes talk about it. I commented that it was clearing up and the sun was coming out, thanked them, and took off.

The ride out of Hawi was all downhill back to Kawaihae, and it went fast. I loved it and thought, Just keep it steady and pick up some speed here. Once it flattened out again, the ocean was on my right. I was still on a high from the downhill, plus all the B vitamins, caffeine, sugar, and ginseng in my Rockstar. I knew I needed something to think about. I began reflecting about every person who had helped me in my journey to Kona. I thought of every detail about each person—their smile, face, laugh, idiosyncrasies, everything I knew about them. As I was doing this, I could feel everyone's prayers and love like a big wave washing over me. I felt enormous energy and gratitude and looked at the God-made beauty surrounding me. I wanted to savor and treasure every minute of it. I thanked God over and over for bringing me to Kona and for all the people who had been instrumental in helping me get here. I started to cry with joy and it was at that moment this picture was taken, so perfectly timed. I'll always remember exactly what I was thinking at the time—making this photo a huge keepsake for me.

Karen biking by the water — Kona

Next, I came to some rolling hills where I met a woman handing out red popsicles in plastic store-bought bags. They were like the kind I ate from the convenience store when I was a kid. Her car was parked on the side of the highway and she and her son were giving them out of a cooler they had next to them. Without even thinking, I stopped and ate one. It was so good. The ice and sugar tasted so yummy and helped cool me off. I thanked her profusely and went on, still holding one half. It started melting and became a big mess, so I took one more bite and tossed the rest. Then it hit me what a huge mistake that could have been. What if it didn't agree with me, or what if she had added something to it?

As quickly as the thought came up, I dismissed it, knowing my mind was getting carried away. The popsicle was simply a bit of fun for me to enjoy.

Further on, a man on a homemade scooter in the middle of the highway was playing a kiddie guitar hooked up to an amplifier. I had no idea where the power source was—there was nothing around for miles. I cheered for him and laughed. He had made that stretch of the ride more enjoyable.

As I rode from the red dirt to the black lava fields, I was getting closer to the Energy Lab and Kona for the run. There were far fewer messages on the white rocks on this side of the highway, and as I was noticing that very thing, I saw a rock sculpture of a tyrannosaurus rex that astounded me. At first, I thought maybe I was delirious from fatigue and was seeing things. How could there be a rock sculpture of a T-rex out here? I did a double take and rubbed my eyes. It was still there. I laughed aloud because of an ongoing joke that Crystal had shared. She'd been teasing me that I was a T-rex texter. She had found a graphic of a T-Rex with short arms texting on a big phone, because I had just gotten a new Samsung Galaxy 3 that had a big screen, which pushed my arms back to my sides when I held it in front of me to text. I couldn't wait to tell her and drive back later to show it to her and the other Sistas.

I came up a hill and saw a female athlete about 60 years old, stopped with a flat bike tire. A male athlete had stopped to help her, and she was trying to call for race maintenance to help. I stopped and asked if I could assist, and the gentleman helping her asked if I had a co2 cartridge adapter. I did and got it out of my bag. He put it on a co2 cartridge and on the stem of her tire to fill it up. The air wasn't going in; they had gone through several cartridges and her tire was still flat. From the minute she got off the phone calling for bike support, she was negative, saying, "I haven't seen any maintenance support people all day!" I told her I had seen many and had just passed a van 10 minutes ago or so. She told me this was not her first race here, after which I wondered why she didn't know, first of all, that no cell phones were allowed on the course and, second, that race support traveled the course on a continuous basis. She kept getting uglier and more negative, so I said, "Well, I'm sorry I can't do more for you. When I see the next support vehicle, I will tell him you need help. Good luck." I couldn't leave fast enough. I couldn't understand how someone could be so negative in this race with all this beauty everywhere. I couldn't even fathom complaining on this day, but I had no idea how much more of it I would hear.

I was bombarded with strong headwinds during the last 30 miles in between the swanky hotels and the Natural Energy Lab, but I got through it. I started seeing age groupers who were already headed for the finish on their run, and it made me feel a little slow. Some of them looked terrible and others looked fine. I wondered what the difference was between the athletes. I listened to songs in my head and worked to remember all of the words. It worked like a charm to keep me sharp and help me maintain a steady pace. I was mentally sharp the whole time and told a lot of people "Good job" as I passed them. It made me feel good and I wanted the encouragement to help them. I concentrated on the course and thought of my own race. This was my journey and nobody else's.

I rode from the Queen K into town and down the hill to the transition area. I saw Ruby and Crystal, who were cheering for me and I pumped my arm in victory and blew them a kiss. Once at the entry to the transition area, I dismounted and handed off my bike to a volunteer (who would re-rack it for me, another thing that never happened in other races), and ran to the gear bag tent to get my run bag, then back to the transition tent. They took the bag and sat me down on the chairs again. They asked if I needed medical attention, food, water, gel, or anything else. Again I asked, "What can I get?" Among the things they listed was an ART (Active Release Therapy) massage. I immediately took them up on it, asking the therapist to massage my right calf, which was sore and extremely tight. I had had good results from doing an ART series with a licensed ART therapist in Denver, so I knew this would help. While the therapist massaged my calf, the other volunteers changed my shoes and socks, took off my cooling sleeves, put more sunscreen on, and changed out my hat and race belt for my run belt, which had gels and glucose tablets in it for the run. I used the port-o-potty, and again, didn't want to leave transition. Everyone was so nice and helpful. I thought, Okay, time to finish this thing and run my marathon.

The crowd was going crazy as I ran out of the tent, and Ruby and Crystal had changed positions so we could high-five each other on my way out. I told them I felt absolutely wonderful and had so many things to share with them from the bike course. They said good luck and to kick ass. Then I heard Mike Reilly announce,

"And there goes Karen Brown of team Sistas to complete her run. Let's wish her well."

The running leg of the course first took us through 10 miles of town out of the 26.2 miles of the race before heading out to the highway. One of the Sistas ran with me for one mile, on the other side of barricades—not on the racecourse. Then she stopped and said she would pick me back up when I came by to head out to the Queen K. I was alone and enjoyed running through the parts of town I had biked and run prior to race day. There were people cheering and watching from their houses and condos along the road. A beautiful full moon as big as the earth came out as I watched and watched a gorgeous sunset that seemed to last forever. I thought it fittingly beautiful to mark this part of the race in my mind. It was punctuating the end of one of the most magnificent days of my life. Everything seemed at peace: my thoughts, my feelings, and my body. All was the way it should be, and I felt an ease in what I was doing. Not that it was easy, just that I was in the flow of it and felt as if I was one with the earth, the ocean, the sun, the moon and, therefore, Spirit.

As I went by the other athletes, I talked to them if an opportunity arose. When I did so with one guy, we struck up a conversation. He lived in Hawaii, and was going to helicopter school. His name was Greg. We ran together for two miles and it was great to have someone to talk to and get out of the isolation of being in my head. I would ask him short questions that I knew would take him a while to answer so I wouldn't have to talk. Even though I was conserving my energy by not talking, I felt really great and strong.

During mile 5 of the run I came across the first aid station with the famous chicken soup. Having chicken soup at aid stations along the marathon course started somewhere in the history of Ironman and became part of the lore that athletes handed down from year to year. The advice was to take the chicken soup because it provides much needed sodium and carbohydrates at a critical time when your body is depleted. It also just plain tastes good, maybe reminding us of comfort food when we are sick and chicken soup is the cure. The theory is that if it makes you feel good when you are sick, maybe it will do the same for you in the race.

The volunteers offered it to me and I refused, not wanting it to upset my stomach—but it smelled really good. Lots of athletes were taking it, along with the bread they provided. I wanted to stay on track and didn't want anything to derail me. I finally reached the run turnaround and headed back to the center of town, at which point I would be 10 miles in, with only 16 to go out the Queen K and back to the finish. I thought, Wow, this is so doable!

I didn't like that it was getting dark, but there was nothing I could do about it. I kept going. Pretty soon, I reached my Sista again who had run with me and this consuming thought came over me. I asked her to call Glenn for me to let him know I was okay. I needed to call Glenn before I was out on the Queen K. Glenn was surprised to hear from her about me. He immediately thought something must be wrong. I hadn't even thought of that. I told her to tell him I was doing great, had had a beautiful day and was feeling strong and that I had noticed the time and wanted to call before I wouldn't be able to. He was astounded.

This is what I was thinking and was able to tell him later, which brought tears to his eyes: I had thought of a song that reflected our relationship and reminded me of something he had said to me earlier about loving me immeasurably. When he had said it, I said it back and thought I recognized the line from somewhere, but couldn't place it. It had taken me almost all day on the bike thinking about it to figure it out. It is a song by Rod Stewart called "You're In My Heart." I told him this, and there was a pause. He told me he was moved at my gesture of that phone call during the biggest event of my life.

Having talked to Glenn through my Sista, I felt elated and energized for the final leg of the race. I made my way up Palani Drive, which is a well-known hill approaching the Queen K. As I ran up it, a man crossed the street who struck me as being someone of significance. He was tall and thin, dressed in a white dress shirt, black short pants, and a thin black tie, with longish crazy hair. He was completely out of place there. The crowds lined each side and, even though it was a public street, not a single person was crossing so as not to impede athletes. Except for this guy. He was just striding, big-as-you-please, across the street, right in my way. Could he not see I had a race bib on? I almost ran into him as he crossed the street and I gave him a hard time. After that, I said, "Hey, who are you, by the way?" He turned and said, "Angus Young of AC/DC." I freaked out and hugged him and said how I loved the band. A spectator said, "He's not Angus Young!" And as I ran off, I told the spectator to be quiet. After this, I just kept laughing to myself and finding surprise in the entertainment that was in this race. I was now headed onto the Queen K highway, had completed 10 miles of the marathon, and knew I only had 16 to go to finish this entire race. That thought was really exciting to me!

As I ran on the Queen K, it grew completely dark, and the amber streetlights came on. They were spaced pretty far apart, and it became hard to see the street. It hit me all at once how many athletes fall during this part of the race. I had seen it happen on TV countless times. I wished I had my headlamp and knew it was waiting for me at the Energy Lab, which was 17.3 miles into the marathon. I set my focus on getting there. The water stations were really fun at this point. There were spaced approximately every mile. The volunteers had decorated them with lots of lights and movement and loud music. It was great—like running into a small concert—and the volunteers were extremely positive and supportive.

At one of the water stations, I decided to try a little bit of the chicken soup to get something in my empty stomach. It's not that I was running out of energy. I had plenty. My stomach just felt completely and utterly empty. The soup tasted really good, was the perfect temperature, and had the right amount of salt. I was careful not to eat too much. I had a few sips and then I continued to the next station. It was a mile between each one, so I focused on running the entire mile, even if it was at a slow pace, and then walking through the aid stations to get water and take a gel or glucose before running again. When I stopped for a bit longer, I immediately felt my muscles start to stiffen, so I kept moving.

I started to come across athletes I had passed on the bike and struck up brief conversations about how great their day was and things like that. I was again struck by how negative so many athletes were; even those I knew had completed the race the year before. I vowed to keep my mind positive. Finally, I got to make the turn into the Energy Lab. I had so looked forward to this. I'd seen it for 30 years on television and knew that for competitors it meant the home stretch to the finish. What I didn't realize was that we had to run all the way into the Energy Lab before the turnaround and the special needs area that had the bag with my headlamp in it. I quickly realized that the station wasn't set up halfway through the run; it was more like two-thirds, 17.3 of the 26.2 miles. It was also darker in that area because of fewer streetlights. I had to concentrate on picking up my feet with each step to be sure not to trip over some rise in the pavement that I couldn't detect. I saw many people fall prey to this because they were tired and basically shuffling their feet. Each one got up again and I was relieved to see that indomitable spirit.

When I reached mile 22, the sky was dark and full of bright stars. I was running along, thanking every part of my body for doing such a great job of holding up and not only getting me to Kona but also completing it. I systematically sent love to each part of my body and, as I was doing so, I looked up at the sky and saw a shooting star. It was just before a water station and when I got there, I asked a volunteer if they had seen it. The volunteer said, "No, it was meant for you." I knew he was right and continued on, in awe of what I had seen and what it meant to me.

As I ran and passed volunteers, I thanked and clapped for them and for the police officers as often as I could. People rode past on bikes to see the final runners in the night and I called out to them, thanking them for being there and supporting us. As I ran up the last

Karen running — Kona

hill toward town, I could hear the announcer and the crowd two miles away at the finish. The athletes I was running next to were complaining about the last hill and I couldn't take it anymore. I turned around in frustration and yelled, "Really?! You are complaining that God put a hill here—something you can't do anything about. We've gone 138 miles, with only two more to go, and YOU ARE

COMPLAINING?!?" I had a burst of energy and left them in the dust. I took off, pumping my arms and dying to get to the finish line and realize my dream. As I continued, I drew more energy from the huge crowd, knowing that the announcer would be saying my name soon as I crossed the line. I checked my watch and it was going on 10:30 p.m. I had been racing since 7 a.m.—some 15 hours—and I felt great.

There was a firefighter from Wisconsin who had been behind me the entire run. He was running in full fire gear (except for the oxygen tank and mask) to raise money for the first responder 9-11 victims. I was proud to be running into town right in front of him and applauded his performance and heart. As I came down Palani Drive and turned onto a street that parallels Alii, I saw hundreds of people that had thunder sticks, the long plastic tubes you clap together at sporting events. The noise was like being in a large stadium full of people. I could no longer hear myself breathe, just like when I was running the Bolder Boulder. I swear I could feel the ground swelling and moving with all of the energy bouncing around. All the multi-story buildings had people jammed onto every balcony. All of them were cheering and clapping, blowing whistles, air horns, megaphones, ringing tons of cowbells and using anything that made sound that could cheer on the athletes. There were spectators lining both sides of the street in costumes, many with signs of inspiration in general and for specific athletes, some of them amusing. The last 1.5 miles, the road surface was packed full of chalk messages and pictures. As I increased my pace, I couldn't read all of them, and it was okay because it felt like they—along with the spectators—were surrounding me with love and energy. I felt I was one with all of the people and that they were sharing this moment with me, too. It was so fun! I ran faster and faster, and as I turned onto Alii Drive near Lava Java (the energetic, popular local coffee shop where a lot of Ironman athletes, fans, and pros hang out), the crowd turned into thousands and I couldn't hear myself breathe. Everyone was cheering for me and I held my hands up in victory as I ran. It felt like I was floating and I had a level of happiness and joy I had never known. Race photographers clicked away, taking my photo as I went by, and I smiled big and proud as I relished the moments I had been looking forward to through two years of tough training and through 30 years of watching the event on TV before that.

As I made the final turn toward the finish line, Mike Reilly announced, "And here comes Karen Brown of Team Sistas, who says this is her lifelong dream and she is just an ordinary person doing something extraordinary." Then he said the words that every aspiring Ironman can't wait to hear: their name and status.

"Karen Brown of Littleton, Colorado, YOU ARE AN IRONMAN." When Mike Reilly said that, I began to cry. I cried because of so many emotions: joy and happiness to have completed my lifelong dream; relief that the two years of training and stretching myself and an extremely long day were over; recognition of how far I had come; gratitude for getting here and all of the people who played a part in that journey; sorrow for everything I had sacrificed in getting here; and pride that I could finally look myself in the eye knowing I had brought out that feeling that I could be more than I had ever been. I had unlocked it and felt more comfortable in my skin than ever before. I also couldn't wait to share every detail of the day with the Sistas. I threw the last gel from my race belt so that I could get a good photo as I crossed the line. I wanted to show my absolute elation as I crossed and had been thinking all day about what other pro and non-pro athletes had done as they crossed.

Spontaneously, I jumped as high as I could, across the line, which ended up being about 3 feet in the air! As I jumped, I crossed the finish line and thought of my loved ones and all the love I felt that day. I was laughing and crying at the same time and thought how blessed I was to have had this chance to pursue and realize my Kona dream. I took in every second of that day, knowing God had led me there and made every opportunity possible. Every ounce of sweat and every day I struggled were worth it.

Volunteers waited in the finish area to "catch" athletes and walk through everything—in case anyone felt disoriented. But I was as clear as a bell. The volunteers took my timing chip and asked if I wanted to keep my strap. Of course I wanted to! The volunteers put a towel around me and graced me with a beautiful purple lei. Ruby and Crystal came rushing over and embraced me. We hugged and laughed and cried together, and they congratulated me on finishing and jumping across the line. They were surprised to see me do it since they weren't sure what condition I would be in. They asked if I had heard what Mike Reilly said as I was finishing and I was crying, saying yes, I heard him. I knew

Karen hopping over finish line — Kona

they had told him, which is why he had said it. I told them I felt like a celebrity because of them and I loved them so much.

The other Sistas came over and hugged and kissed me. Now, in addition to the orange shirts they had been wearing all day, I saw that they had donned

Karen after crossing finish line — Kona

novelty, light-up white multi-colored bunny ears, so that I could see them easily in the dark. I laughed and thanked them for supporting, loving, and cheering for me. Ruby had brought my recovery drink and I drank some, along with some green smoothie, and then we all posed for a photo. All of us had raccoon eye sunburns from the day and I was proud of them!

Formal race finish photo — Kona

I was sore, tired, and tremendously pumped up, all at the same time. Everyone wanted to share their experiences from the day with each other, and I had to go collect my bike and gear from transition before we could make our way home. Even though my first thought was to eat, it wasn't possible. My stomach had shrunk so much from only having liquids that my body wasn't ready to process food. Some of my friends who ate food on the bike or run ended up throwing up. I never wanted to have to stop and throw up so I had thought it would be better to keep moving and not worry about getting sick.

Ironman had a full spread of food out after the race. There were Hawaiian doughnuts, ham, pizzas, French fries, and chocolate milk. I remember reading in Chrissie Wellington's A Life Without Limits that she had pigged out on two pizzas and 16 doughnuts after her race! After two years of training, I knew my body well enough to know that I wouldn't be able to tolerate the food that was being offered. After the buffet, athletes are sent to be processed out and get their "goodies."

I went to another tent where they took my race number and gave me my finisher bag with a t-shirt, a commemorative refrigerator-magnet timer with my finish time on it, and my finisher medal. But there was no medal in my bag. They had run out of medals by the time that I got there. Part of the medals got misrouted and they assured me they would get my medal to me later, possibly while I was still on the island after the race. After I got my bag, my volunteer and I went to a small podium with a backdrop; professional photos were taken of each finisher with their medal. Normally, they would snap the picture of the athlete right away, but it was taking a while to coordinate where I was staying and when they could get my medal to me. I lay down and stretched because I could feel my muscles becoming stiff. I was still beaming as I stretched, and I felt a deep sense of purpose and satisfaction at what I had accomplished. A nice man from Australia came over and gave me pointers on how to stretch more effectively, and he let me take a photo with his medal.

I had to walk back to transition to collect my bike and two gear bags, although that was the last thing I wanted to do. I just wanted to be carried home and fall into bed! The transition area was still athletes-only, so I was slow in getting my stuff and walked ever so slowly back to the spectator area in front of the King Kamehameha Hotel. I was going to meet up with the Sistas to go back to the condo. Cut-off time is midnight and it was about 11:15 pm, which meant the crowd was waiting to see the final finishers become Ironmen along with the pros who had finished a long while ago. It is customary for the winning male and female to wait at the finish line and congratulate the last finishers of the day and crown them Ironmen.

After I finally gathered my bag from that morning with the stuff that I took off before the swim, I walked very deliberately back up to where the Sistas were—exactly the same place I had left them almost 16 hours earlier. I wasn't shuffling, but I was certainly very sore and could tell stiffness and swelling were already starting. Once I got to them, we hugged, re-united again, and immediately worked out our plan to get back to the condo as quickly as possible. I was so happy to be finished, and my mind was very clear. I had a huge sense of satisfaction and couldn't stop smiling. Since there had been no place to park because of the number of people, we had left the rental car back at the condo and needed to hail a cab. Problem was the only cab we could catch was two blocks up the hill—where we had just been! It was really hard for me to walk up a simple hill! I sucked it up and walked up the hill to the cab. I was grateful it was a mini-van since I could get my bike inside, and the Sistas all helped put my gear in and get me situated.

After we got back to the condo, we were all so pumped up that we couldn't go to bed. We stayed up for two hours, sharing all of our individual experiences from the day. They shared how the announcer saw them first thing and asked about the bright orange shirts, and how they told him my story, not knowing he would use every detail they told him. I told them about the magical things that happened during the day: seeing Julie Moss and Kathleen McCartney, the T-rex rock sculpture, the guitar guy on the highway, Angus Young, and seeing the shooting star. I think they wondered if I had lost my marbles during the race. We laughed and hugged and had a jovial time and, finally, at 2 a.m., we all went our separate ways. As we ended the day, I kept saying to myself, "I did it! I did it! It is done!" I think my brain was still going 100 miles an hour from all of the energy gels and natural body chemicals like adrenaline and endorphins that had pumped through me all day. I had a hard time calming down enough to feel like going to bed, and then I couldn't sleep for a long while because I couldn't get comfortable. My entire body ached, and my immune system was so depleted I felt feverish. I used compression socks and Ibuprofen, which helped the swelling and aches, but nothing took the pain away completely.

The process of going to bed after an Ironman is this: shower and get off what feels like 100 pounds of grime, dust, sun, wind, and rain. My skin felt like sandpaper and so did my eyes, even though I wore sunglasses all day. Then, I applied aloe vera on the sunburned parts of my body—legs from halfway down my quads to ankles where my socks were, back and shoulders where the sun beat down on me all day, and my hands. Since I didn't bike with gloves, my hands were the most sunburned. My skin where I had worn my watch and Ironman bracelet was white as could be. I attempted more stretching but was very stiff. I kept trying to drink as much water as possible. Once I lay down in bed, I tossed and turned for two hours, not being able to turn off all the thoughts about what had happened during the race. Things that I had forgotten about earlier were now all coming back to me like a movie reel. The thing that finally did help me sleep was praying to God with immense gratitude for all of the joy, light, and grace during the day.

The Ironman tent opened at 7 a.m. the next morning so racers could get their finisher merchandise. Since we didn't get to bed until 2 a.m. and I knew I wouldn't be able to sleep much and would be sore and stiff the next day, going to the tent for the merchandise wasn't high on my list of priorities. We decided to sleep in and go get a nice breakfast. I figured that whatever finisher stuff they had left when I sauntered in was meant for me, and the Sistas agreed.

I tossed and turned until 10 a.m. and then got up. The Sistas were up and about, and we mobilized to go get a good breakfast. My throat was sore from the salt water, and would be for the next two days, but it was not as bad as others had told me it would be. The swelling I had read about started fast. Several articles and Chrissie Wellington's book talked about swelling in your legs the days after the race. None said the cause, just that it happened. Bob Cranny told me later it's caused by a failure of the Venous Return system, which allows your veins to push blood back up your legs to your heart. Because of the long hours of the day and being vertical for so many of them, that system just fails until it can repair itself over a few days. From my waist down, I was a full size larger. I was okay walking slowly, but stairs were a bit sketchy and hurt to go up or down. We drove into town and found a place overlooking the bay to eat; we had a long wait for breakfast because every place was packed. We finally got a table and I ordered pancakes, an omelet, hash browns, and toast. I was intensely hungry and I couldn't wait to satisfy my hunger with the great food that I had thought about during the race. Think about it—going for 15 hours exercising and not eating. While we waited for the food, I was in and out of lucidity. We talked and laughed and the Sistas told me later that I would say something that made sense and then something that was pure nonsense. I still felt feverish and was sure my body was trying to recover from the immense exertion of the day before.

The food came and we all dug in. I ate maybe five bites and my stomach was absolutely stuffed and started to hurt. I put my fork down, very disappointed. Ruby asked if I was okay and I told her that was all that would fit in my stomach. She nodded in understanding and said it would be okay to wait a while until I would be able to eat more. It was a weird, scary feeling, knowing my body needed nutrients badly and not being able to eat. After almost an hour, I was able to shove down two more bites, but that was it. My stomach hurt and I surmised it was stretching and straining to process the food. I had never had that feeling before and it was a bit unnerving.

We made our way to the finisher merchandise tent. Since we got there late, the huge crowds had dissipated a bit. We all scattered to find the things meaningful to each of us to mark the event. We spent 90 minutes in the tent, grabbing things, putting them back, and grabbing other things, until finally each of us had our "pile of stuff" to purchase. There was a long line to check out and Ruby noticed that my body swelling was getting worse the longer I was on my feet. My skin started to hurt because it was stretched so much. Ruby grabbed my stuff and told me to go sit down and she would take care of it for me. I went and sat on the curb and watched as the Sistas made our purchases.

There were so many errand-type things going on in the days after the race that required me to walk (athlete awards banquet, coordinating pick-up of my finisher medal and official Ironman photos, etc.) that I had no choice but to walk, which caused more swelling. I would get so swollen below the waist that my skin would hurt again. The finisher pictures were in. I didn't even remember until a friend mentioned it to me. By the time we got there for pick-up, they were closed, and then they were gone the following day. We also had to go to the Ironman office in another part of the hotel to coordinate getting my finisher medal, which meant more walking! It was a bit of a whirlwind that left me feeling like the time after the race was a blur, but it was also incredibly fun—even if running errands was the last thing I wanted to do. That night the banquet of champions was held, but I was too exhausted to go.

My stomach took an entire month to bounce back, which was the oddest feeling. I wanted to eat because I knew I needed nutrition and calories, but eating more than a few bites of food made me feel full. If I overate, my stomach would swell up and become distended and my ribs would hurt. It felt like my food was sitting in my stomach and backing up into my esophagus. Then as my stomach would work to digest the food, it felt like a shuddering or trembling sensation. I started wondering what had happened to my system and if an emergency-room visit would be on the horizon. Ruby and Crystal assured me I would be okay, and it would simply take time. Even though they didn't really know, I didn't question what they said. Drinking green smoothies helped, but my stomach couldn't keep up with solid food. If there is a next time for me, I'll know to eat small meals frequently so that I can stop for a while if my stomach can't keep up.

What I realized during this period was how I wanted to use this experience to help others. I had kept notes of everything that had happened along the way in all of my races and training, and the idea of this book came to me. Maybe I could share my story with large groups of people and show them that they, too, are capable of anything they set their minds to. They just have to decide to do it. Maybe they could see that anything, truly anything, is possible. That is also the Ironman tagline, by the way. The last thought I had was that I felt like I was finally fulfilling my true potential in life. That gut feeling that I could do more had changed. I felt fulfilled and happy, like I was on the right track. Now that I had completed this, what would be the next step?

We stayed in Kona for another week and went for a helicopter ride. Then we drove back to Hawi so I could show them that cute village and the T-rex sculpture I'd seen during the triathlon. I know none of them believed it was actually there, so they all howled when they saw it. We went cliff jumping at the south point of the island and visited beautiful beaches until Crystal, Alicia and Marge all departed. To get the best airfare, they all had flights leaving at different times. So one by one, we hugged and said goodbye, knowing that this was the type of magic that happens once in a lifetime. Ruby and I stayed the longest and had some fun together, just the two of us, which was glorious. I love my sister and really enjoy spending time with her. We went up to Kohala (northeast of Hawi) for a great zip-lining tour through the rainforest canopy. We were thinking of learning to surf and opted for paddle-boarding instead because it seemed a bit safer. It turned out to be way harder than we thought because of the balance needed while paddling on ocean waves. Good paddle-boarders make it look easy! We were definitely teetering but happy that we tried something new. It was the time of my life and I have never been so grateful or felt so close to my sister and my group of women.

In addition to being grateful for these amazing women, I felt an overwhelming, deep gratitude for my coach, Grant. When I crossed the finish line at Kona, I gave him the credit. I knew that Brandon hadn't needed to take me on, especially such a short time before Kona. He helped prevent a more serious injury, and I don't think I would have made it across the finish line without him. I never mentioned Gretchen, and news apparently spread in the coaching world to the point that others were giving Brandon a hard time because he hadn't been my coach that long. Some even tried to get him in trouble for it. But he remained strong, respectful, and transparent. No wrong had been done. I was impressed with how he handled himself, and I am and will be forever grateful for his guidance and support.

The day we left the island was bittersweet. Ruby and I completed the checklist for leaving the condo and went down to the restaurants on Alii Drive where I had run to the finish line days earlier. We ate at a restaurant overlooking the bay where I swam. It was a hot, sunny day with no clouds and no wind. As we sat eating lunch, we talked about our favorite parts of the trip and reflected on how incredible the whole experience was and how fortunate we were to be able to stay for two weeks total. We walked slowly down Alii Drive along the seawall after lunch and I asked Ruby to take a final photo of me in front of the ocean. I had such a feeling of home and belonging that it felt weird to leave. As we got into the car, there was a van parked next to us. In the back window it said: "Your life is a product of the thoughts you think. Live Aloha." I thought, What a perfect end to our time here. As Ruby and I took off from the airport, we looked out the window at all of the places we had been and continued to look until we couldn't see the island any longer. Love filled our hearts and we both sat back to relax and sleep for the journey home. We had lived this experience to the fullest extent possible and were both changed for the better because of it.

Chapter 23

Life After Kona

When I returned to Colorado, I had a deep sense of satisfaction at knowing what I had accomplished in the Ironman. I spent time reflecting on my experiences and my personal growth over the previous two years and thought of everything I had done to get there and what I did to finish. I needed to discover who I was through the process of training and running in triathlons.

Even though I always knew I was capable of big things, I felt like I had been holding back before Kona. I had blamed others for holding me back until I realized what it was to have a victim mentality. When I came to understand that, I started peeling back the layers and understood I was the one holding myself back from accomplishing my goals.

After I accomplished my dream in Kona, one of the agents in my office said I seemed different. She said I was more attentive and softer. It took me time to process that she was right. Through my journey to Kona, I became more comfortable with myself because I knew what I was capable of and had no doubts. As part of my training and my journey, I learned to have faith and trust in the Lord and in the gifts I was given. I started trusting in my own abilities, even when people doubted me.

This journey brought me to where I am today. My beliefs extend beyond my own sense of my world. Call it God, Spirit, or the Universe. A power greater than myself is what I now experience. On a daily basis, faith and trust manifest themselves like this for me: I identify something I want to do, a goal. My first thought is excitement and having a vision of completing it or what it might feel like to complete it. Then I ask what will be needed to complete it and I go over it in my mind. Instead of feeling uneasy, scared, or fearful like I used to about the necessary components I don't have or don't know, I now think Well, I will trust and have faith in God to bring what I need and for what I don't yet know I need to reach my goal. This implicit trust brings me an enormous sense of peace.

Moreover, this process and way of thinking manifests itself daily with being grateful when I wake up in the morning and go to sleep at night. I am grateful for the gifts the day has brought, even if they were challenging.

I used to hold myself back because I didn't know how to do what I wanted—I didn't have the resources or the knowledge, or the money, or whatever else might be needed. I was able to shift my thinking when I decided to pursue Kona. With my dream of Kona, I didn't know what I needed, nor did I have a clue about the first steps in getting there. But the dream was strong! I knew I was holding myself back with my usual arsenal of reasons. With that insight came the understanding that it was up to me to make the decision and then release the outcome. To put it out there to the Universe, Spirit, God, trusting I would receive what I would need. I have also learned that when you make a decision like this and verbalize it, your brain literally starts working on getting it.

I used to worry—a lot. Even after I came into relationship with God, I had a hard time letting my worries go and trusting that I was right where I should be. Over time, enough of my friends kept reinforcing to me, "Lay it at God's feet. It's ultimately in his hands anyway. Your worrying about it is not doing any good." This clicked with me, and I began envisioning letting go of my worries in this way. It became a habit I grew better at over time. When I would feel anxious after worrying myself out, I would worry over a shorter span of time before picturing myself handing it over. This switch in my thinking helped me, much as it helped me when I changed my concept of "the edge of the comfort zone" from being the precipice of a cliff, to an endlessly stretchable rubber band.

We all need to discover what makes life doable for us and how we, as individuals, can live more skillfully. What I found for my own life is that once I stop fighting what I'm feeling, worry transforms into peace and a sense of knowing it's going to be all right. It's going to be taken care of, whether there are minor stumbling blocks or intimidating roadblocks appearing along the way. I'm certainly not perfect at letting go of worry, but since Kona it's easier. I'm less likely to grip onto that old illusion of control. I'm more inclined to respond with initial surprise and then think Okay, apparently there's something I need to learn here. Or someone I need to meet. Or something I didn't need to do, to get where I want to go.

The agent who pointed out that my demeanor had softened also pointed out the magnitude of my accomplishment in comparison to the everyday things people do. That comment opened up my eyes. I used to be scared and uneasy when swimming, and I had been terrified at the mere thought of swimming in an ocean. After training and building my skills, swimming became second nature, and my fears eased. I found it was an exhilarating experience to swim in the open ocean, and I embraced it. It was the same with biking. When I started training, I thought cycling was boring if it wasn't on mountain trails. I couldn't fathom riding for more than 100 miles, but that became common in my training. I grew to enjoy it. In fact, two days after the race, the Sistas and I drove to Hawi and the drive seemed far longer than it had while cycling during the Ironman.

I thought of all the people who had said I couldn't do Kona—and I was proving them wrong. I had known I could, but I had let others create doubts in my mind. I promised myself I wouldn't give others that power again. I was assured and started to relax in more ways than I ever had before. It brought me a feeling of happiness, like the entire world was opened up to me and I was bound by nothing. Maybe this was how ordinary people go on to do extraordinary things.

I learned how to quiet my thoughts and clarify my focus. I had thought I knew how to do this because of practicing yoga, but I wasn't able to focus as much as I thought I would in that practice. I had still experienced a million thoughts running through my mind. When I stopped using the iPod for music, a whole new world opened up to me—a world I never knew existed. Ideas came to me while I was training and I would often jot them down after a long ride or run. Prior to training, this only happened when I was on vacation. I learned to value the time I spent training, because it was time away from the world and its influences. Now the clear thinking is always there; I no longer feel like I'm sacrificing things for training.

Since Kona, my life has continued changing. I learned what is most important. I admit that I was shallow and materialistic before and tended to want attention for what I had and who I was. I believe this came from my insecurities, from not knowing who I really was. Outwardly, I projected a very together person. But the way I felt was small in comparison to who I dared to dream I could be. As I got older it got worse. As I did more, it got worse. It's like an itch you can't scratch. The song "This Is Your Life" by Switchfoot, which is one of my mantra songs, has a lyric that goes, "Are you who you want to be?" This song really got to me: because my answer was always no.

Growing up, I dreamed of becoming a powerful, rich, beautiful, career woman. When I began working, I was out to prove myself to be just that with every job I took. Wanting to be powerful, rich, and beautiful was me wanting attention from others. What I came to understand was that none of that brought happiness. But for a long time I thought it would. I thought the same about primary relationships with men. Because I didn't know who I really was, I would become what each man I set my sights on wanted—only to find out that wasn't really me.

It wasn't until I learned how strong I could be through building a thriving real estate business, pursuing and accomplishing Kona, and helping others that I understood who I was. I then realized that for me, success and happiness meant service—I wanted to help others find their way instead of concentrating on the conventional trappings of success our society pushes. Now, I know who I am. In some ways, I have become more driven than I was before because I know what I'm capable of.

Any time spent not pursuing my capabilities in the ultimate service of others is time wasted. My goals have shifted: I want to tell the world about my experience and help others reach their goals. I've learned to think bigger than I ever did before—in every part of my life. Now, it seems like nothing is out of reach.

I know that I raced in Kona on my own terms. I didn't succumb to people who said I wasn't fast enough or who pressured me to race faster. I had the most beautiful and joyous race day. It would have been a different experience had I raced in a different way. I stayed the course, and I knew at my core that I could do it. I believed in myself when people said I was crazy.

I've learned to become more organized and efficient. Time is efficiency. I always think of what I can do better or more efficiently. This guides me to focus on personal improvement and brings a crystal-clear fluidity toward achieving my goals. I now surround myself with supportive people and enjoy learning from others. I have learned a big lesson: to ask for help as soon as I need it. I also like to think I can bring something to others and make a difference for them. I am, of course, still on a journey of faith, and I continue to learn more about the process in the effort to become a better person.

I find myself doing things I never thought I would do or try, like writing this book. I find I am stepping into new shoes more often by not limiting myself. I never thought I could do the Ironman because I wasn't of a world-class caliber. Now, I think I am world-class because of my mindset and accomplishments.

I'm also considering competing in Ultraman. I first learned about Ultraman in Rich Roll's book. It is a double Ironman, back-to-back over three days. I could never understand how he did it, having started from a tougher place than I had. Rich Roll was a grossly overweight recovering alcoholic who would become winded climbing a few stairs. Once I completed the Ironman and a 10,000-yard swim with my swim team, it hit me. The way he or any other ultra-athlete does it is by continuing to build endurance past Ironman-level distances. When I first read about the Ultraman race, I shook my head back and forth thinking those guys were truly nuts and there was no way I could do that. Now I know it is doable, because I know what I am capable of. I know that if I trained well, I could go further in swimming, biking, and running than I did in the Ironman. It's all in my head, not my body.

Before I raced at Kona, I thought the effort was 90 percent physical, but I learned that it was actually closer to 90 percent mental. The mindset and focus to motivate myself to be a champion has led me to think of success in a different way than I had before. I'm also focusing on other career opportunities. I am now a business/life coach, author and speaker. I live in line with my purpose.

I look forward to a lifetime of fulfilling my potential and helping others to find their path to fulfilling their potential, too. I will speak to large groups of people and know I am making a difference in the lives of others. My journey has been a series of struggles and accomplishments. That is the opportunity we all have.

Chapter 24

Being in the Zone

I began telling you my story by describing my experience with my own struggles and progress in striving to go beyond the edge of my comfort zone.

I'd like to conclude with some remarks about another kind of "zone." You may already be at least somewhat familiar with the concept—the idea of being in "the zone." It's also called "flow," which is my term of preference because it implies a water current carrying me along.

Flow. It's exactly what I was in throughout the entire race in Kona, as well as what I experienced a number of times during my training leading up to that race.

I'd often wondered what, precisely, this phenomenon of flow was. I'd considered it as a form of intense focus. Yet, I knew there was more to it.

There is more, indeed. Flow or being in the zone encompasses being in a heightened state of consciousness. It can happen when someone is doing a task they find intrinsically motivating, new, and/or challenging. Often, it is something that is particularly challenging to them.

Practicing this challenging task on a regular basis is key to flow. Practice makes you want more of the challenge, and practice leads to increased and ongoing feelings of contentment.

I learned this explanation of flow after Kona. It explains to me why I'm happier and more fulfilled now than I was before I began doing things that were big and challenging to me. It's also why I look to do more of what challenges me.

At Kona I experienced a heightened state of awareness in which I was acutely conscious of everything. At the same time, I wasn't making a conscious effort to pay attention to it. It felt like I easily maintained an intense focus on what I was doing—with a total trust, an effortless faith that I would prevail. It was a particular type of connection with life, in which I felt fully engaged with the present moment.

My very first glimpse of flow occurred years earlier as the often-cited "runner's high." In reading up on this phenomenon, I have come to understand runner's high as the first level of flow. For me, runner's high marked the entry to a much bigger experience on my journey.

Whether or not you're a runner, I'm sure you can relate to the experience of having done something where you had an acute level of focus to the extent that it felt like you couldn't make a mistake and everything was coming to you smoothly and naturally. This is flow.

What leads to flow? In short, it's when you're doing something new or at a higher level than before and chemicals are released in your body somewhat like they are when you are in fight or flight. They get your blood pumping and brain working fast. This is the doorway—and without it, you don't get to the experience of flow.

Now, we have statistics and studies to prove how flow works and how to get into it. What I can say is flow was the best-kept secret of top athletes! I never read or talked much about it until I was able to discover it myself and then build on it.

The science of flow tells us that in the brain, many of the biological chemicals released in long or extreme activities—neurotransmitters such as norepinephrine, adrenaline, serotonin, etc.—come together in a perfect storm, creating the biological cocktail to produce flow. This biological cocktail occurs in no other circumstances.

People who use stimulant drugs of any kind are attempting to re-create this experience; however, flow is akin to taking this artificial drug experience and increasing it a thousand-fold. And, there is no negative aftermath or harmful side effect in genuine flow.

Once you've gotten the practice part of a challenge down pat (a key component leading to flow), getting into flow on a regular basis makes you want to attain flow more often. Just as practice makes you want more of the challenge and leads to increased feelings of contentment, so does flow itself lead to increased ongoing contentment, peace, and happiness.

Being in the flow also allows endurance athletes far greater performance because their muscles are doing precisely what the brain is telling them. The athletes can then reach higher and higher levels of performance. The extraordinary reality of flow proves that you can do more than you thought you could—and more than you did before.

Flow encourages you to build on your core passions and intrinsic motivation. It urges you to become the best version of yourself. I completely felt this at Kona and in my training leading up to it. Moreover, the intensity of flow shortens the path to mastering the skills and abilities you're pursuing. You can make markedly faster progress when you're in the flow than you'd otherwise be able to achieve.

For me, flow was as if I managed to turn off feeling in my body and simply concentrate on my mind as though my body had gone on autopilot and my mind remained active. I was able to think about any given number of topics from beginning to end, in one fluid cycle. It seemed like my mind was at a higher level of thinking because fresh thoughts and perceptions would bubble up to awareness. They weren't forced. I would start thinking about a topic and innovative ideas would appear.

When I was training, I came to understand that my best thinking happened while I was in these states. I often said I should have mounted a voice recorder to my bike. On long rides, I would get so many new ideas I would want to remember after the ride. I like to compare this to the common experience of remembering an insightful or helpful dream: You can remember some or most of it, but usually not all the details.

Where do these new ideas and fresh thoughts come from? When you are in flow, you hear "the voice." It is a clear, strong voice communicating ideas to you. Because I am a believer, I always called these my conversations with God. I've mentioned that I prefer the term "flow" because it imparts the idea of being carried along by water; one of the biblical names for God is Yahweh, which translates to "ever flowing." Others call the voice of flow intuition.

The voice can manifest as images or pictures, too—a "visual voice" if you will. In flow, many people, myself included, have experienced personal epiphanies, and a wealth of other types of sudden, intuitive perceptions or insights. This voice, in short, is quite the opposite of the commonplace mind-chatter we all endure in our daily lives.

I've learned to translate flow and the voice of flow to other parts of my life: work, relationships, spirituality, personal development, and more. I know its real power. The difference it has created in my life has been substantial.

What I have found is that the voice is never wrong. When I didn't follow what the voice said is when I didn't perform as well as I could have. The voice feels like the strongest gut feeling I have ever had.

Flow: I think of it as palpable, tangible. Flow allows you to feel at one with nature, or perhaps have a sense of unity with your racing equipment. In Kona, I felt like I was an extension of the bike, or perhaps the bike was an extension of me. I enjoyed the same feeling swimming in the ocean and running on the course. I felt one with the water, one with the road, like it was my heavenly home on earth. Even in the dark, I felt my way when others were falling. That is the energy and synergy of flow.

What gets you into the flow of your life?

I'd like to leave you with a personal challenge. Spend some time thinking about your deeply held dreams, goals, and ambitions. Ask yourself the private questions you may have gotten into the habit of avoiding. Confronting yourself can be scary, so be gentle and compassionate with yourself as you proceed. Over the course of my Kona experience, I've come to think that we make decisions about our abilities and capabilities at an unconscious level, and then we accept those decisions as fact rather than as stories we've told ourselves. I think this is so common that it's most likely simply a part of being human.

Our core beliefs can be very powerful, yet most of the time we're not even aware that beliefs are just ideas we choose to accept. For each of us, our own uniquely developed core beliefs dictate our behaviors more often than not. Our own scripts and stories, including opinions, judgments, and other thoughts of who we see ourselves as, can limit and restrict us. I believe many times we're not even totally aware of our own agendas and motives behind our reasons for not living life on our terms.

The next time you find yourself dismissing a goal with the defeatist thought that you can't achieve it anyway because "That's just the way things are" or hear someone else echoing those sentiments, I challenge you to ask yourself, "Says who?" Do this as a reminder that you can choose to stop agreeing to the stories about your limitations. Instead of asking "Why?" ask "Why not?" You can decide not to accept the social agreements and collective assumptions so many of us quietly internalize and accept as fact. Who, after all, is deciding for us whether it's sensible or practical or realistic to pursue a goal we hold dear? Why would we let someone else decide for us that it's time we put aside our dreams? This "someone else" includes our own minds—because our minds never stop telling us stories about how we'll fail if we try.

We've been seduced into believing we should view failure as a possibility or as an inevitability, or failure as a valid reason for delaying our dreams. But what is failure, other than the way we sort out what will prove helpful or unhelpful to us as we continue to reach for what we want? I remember the Thomas Edison quote: "I have not failed 700 times. I have not failed once. I have succeeded in proving that those 700 ways will not work. When I have eliminated the ways that will not work, I will find the way that will work." Failure is simply a facet of success. It's not a personal indictment of your innate potential. It's your right to follow your heart's desire—the creative, the artistic, the intellectual, the physical, the emotional, the spiritual endeavors that call to you are yours to savor. Give yourself permission to reclaim your power to do so.

Based on my experiences while pursuing my goal of Kona, I'd like to offer you a few fundamentals for getting started on pursuing your own goals. First, allow yourself to reframe the notion of comfort zone. It's a counterfeit comfort, a fake. It's really a wall we construct to keep ourselves stuck and hold ourselves back. There's nothing comforting about that, is there? See that comfort zone for what it truly is: a self-constructed prison. Don't beat yourself up for not realizing you put yourself in prison and had the key to release yourself from it the whole time.

Next, think about what you want out of life. Think about the values you want to live by and the goals your heart wants you to pursue. It's the pursuing that really comprises the joy. Reaching a goal constitutes a nice by-product of the pursuit. But it's the quest and journey that satisfy the soul. And by all means, maintain a healthy sense of humor! Take your goals seriously, but take yourself lightly.

Finally, think about those times you've experienced being in the zone or flow, where you are so engrossed in what you're doing that you lose track of time. Fresh thoughts and perceptions enter your consciousness of their own accord. When does that happen for you? If you're not sure, start journaling about it. Ask your closest friends for their insights. Being in flow offers you views into your most sacred yearnings in life.

What do you suspect might bring joy to your heart? Little things or big things or anything in-between…. It's such an intimately personal matter. Perhaps it's something you've been putting off for years but would like to try. Maybe it's something you've been told (and told yourself) you weren't capable of doing or shouldn't do. Again, ask yourself: "Says who?" Or possibly, it's something you've attempted at various times in your life but didn't quite follow through on, or didn't complete to your satisfaction. Whatever the answers you uncover, you have today to begin anew. Now is your moment to identify with the inner power you possess. We're meant to flow with life; we're intended for our distinctive journey here on Earth. I know you can realize your true potential.

What's your Kona? Follow your path to self! I send you blessings along your way!

ABOUT THE AUTHOR

Karen Brown relentlessly pursued and ultimately realized her dream of completing the Ironman World Championships in Kona, HI, unlocking her potential in life.

What is your potential? What is the key to unlocking it? What will pursuing it do for you and your life? Every one of us has gifts and talents, and we are capable of so much more than we realize.

Karen is available to speak to community and corporate groups, and offers TED-style talks as well as keynote addresses. She and her company, Velocity Leadership Consulting, offer one-on-one business psychology coaching for individuals and corporate partners, velocity leadership workshops, webinars and podcasts.

Velocity Leadership Consulting
1-800-217-0017
www.velocityleadershipconsulting.com
info@velocityleadershipconsulting.com

What Karen has been up to since Ironman World Championships

Karen relishes in setting and achieving new challenges that expand her potential. Below are some recent events and accomplishments:

- Made History: Ultraman Canada Crew Director for the first double-amputee to complete the race—2013
- Ultraman World Championships—2014 (by invitation only)
- Ironman Texas—2014 (bettered Kona finish time by 2 hours)
- Holualoa Marathon—2015 (first 4-hour marathon time, to qualify for Comrades)
- Ultra 520K Canada (formerly Ultraman)—2015 (by invitation only)
- Comrades Ultra Marathon, South Africa—2016
- Delivered keynote speech to a crowd of 300 in South Africa—2016
- Leadville 100 MTB—2016 (did not finish)
- UTMB: Training for Ultra Trail Mont Blanc—2018 (this now requires up to a three-year qualification process)
- Writing books Two and Three on change and the role it plays in success, and the truth about nutrition and health.
- Spent three days with legendary Brian Tracy, who endorsed her book
- Became certified Master Practitioner, Neuro-Linguistic Programming, using the power of the unconscious mind for greater success in your business and personal life.

Morgan James
Speakers Group

www.TheMorganJamesSpeakersGroup.com

We connect Morgan James published authors with live and online events and audiences who will benefit from their expertise.

Morgan James makes all of our titles available
through the Library for All Charity Organization.

www.LibraryForAll.org

Printed in the USA
CPSIA information can be obtained
at www.ICGtesting.com
JSHW022323140824
68134JS00019B/1261

9 781683 504160